NEW POEMS

(1968–1970)

OTHER WORKS BY PABLO NERUDA

TRANSLATED AND EDITED BY BEN BELITT

PUBLISHED BY GROVE PRESS

A New Decade (Poems 1958–1967)

Selected Poems of Pablo Neruda

PABLO NERUDA

NEW POEMS
(1968-1970)

**Edited, Translated and
with an Introduction by
Ben Belitt**

008379

GROVE PRESS, INC.   NEW YORK

ISBN: 0–394–48286–7

Library of Congress Catalog Card Number: 72–3709

First Printing

Manufactured in the United States of America
by American Book–Stratford Press, New York

Distributed by Random House, Inc., New York

Some of these translations have appeared in the following periodicals: *The New Yorker:* "Falling," "The Enemy," "Song With A Landscape and A River," "On the Road"; *The Virginia Quarterly Review:* "Silence," "Unity," "A Falling Flower," "Water," "Reason," "Tree," "Animal," "Bees: II," "Dog," "Another Dog," "Fish," "Bestiary: I," "Autumn"; *Audience:* "Casa de Mantares, Punte del Este," "The Bell-Ringer"; *Mundus Artium:* "Other Gods," "Semen," "The Blow"; *The Bennington Silo:* "Beetle." The introductory essay was delivered at the Conference on Contemporary Latin American Literature (University of Houston, March 17–18, 1972) and appears in their anthology, published by the University of Houston Press.

[–B.B.]

For Margaret Ross Burkhardt

Contents

The Moving Finger and the Unknown Neruda

It has been the fate of moving talents to offer stationary targets to partisan and provincial readers. Neruda belongs with Protean spirits like Blake ("The cistern contains: the fountain overflows") and Yeats, who threw his mythological coat to the dogs and chose to "walk naked." Until recently, the erosion of Pablo Neruda has been confined to his South American critics, of friendly and hostile persuasions: indeed, the attempt of Neruda to keep his vision large in a diminishing world has been a constant theme of his *oeuvre* during the last two decades. Between the pedantic and political decantations of his expositors he has interposed an apparatus designed to deflect—at strategic intervals—the Trojan gifts of the "experts." His principal weapons have been three: enigma, caprice, and a Socratic epistemology of "ignorance" which resolutely rejects all vested outcomes, including the dialectical fatalism of the Marxist. As early as 1950, he took pains, in a work devoted for the most part to the historical and geological recovery of a public universe, to infiltrate a poem called "The Enigmas" (*Los enigmas*), as a kind of spiritual watermark:

> I am that net waiting emptily—out of range
> of the onlooker, slain in the shadows,
> fingers inured to a triangle, a timid
> half-circle computed in oranges.
>
> Probing a starry infinitude
> I came like yourselves
> through the mesh of my being, in the night, and awoke
> to my nakedness—

Pablo Neruda / xiii

all that was left of the catch, a fish in the noose of
    the wind.

With the increasing polarization of his critics, Neruda has
had to adopt increasingly Daedalian measures, inventing
whole labyrinths, like the unplaceable *Book of Vagaries* (*Es-
travagario*, 1958), from which there is no rational exit, to out-
wit his tidiers. In that extraordinary funhouse of metaphysi-
cal pratfalls, he has curved all the mirrors with illusions
designed to dismay the gullible with parabolic distortions of
their own meddlesome intrusions:

> I would know nothing, dream nothing:
> who will teach my non-being
> how to be, without striving to be?
>
>   (*Estación Inmóvil*)

or:

> I must wait for myself, as they wait for me there:
> I also would see myself coming
> and know in the end how it feels to me
> when I come back to the place where I wait for my
>   coming
> and turn back to my sleep, and die laughing.
>
>   (*Pastoral*)

or:

> I don't know which way to be—
> absent-minded or respectful;
> shall I yield to advice
> or tell them outright they're hysterical?
> Independence, it's clear, gets me nowhere.
> I get lost in the underbrush,
> I don't know if I'm coming or going.
> Shall I take off or stand firm,
> buy tomatoes or tomcats?
>
>   (*Partenogénesis*)

or finally:

> I'll figure out as best I can
> what I ought *not* to do—and then do it . . .
> if I don't make mistakes
> who'll believe in my errors? . . .
> I'll change my whole person . . .
> and then when I'm different
> and no one can recognize me
> I'll keep doing the same things I did,
> since I couldn't possibly do otherwise.
>
> (*Partenogénesis*)

Most recently, the Congress of Swedish Academicians (1971) have enlisted a homogenized Neruda: "For poetry that, with the action of an elemental force, brings alive a continent's destiny and dreams." The Nobel citation serves to chisel into the steles of posterity, like a Roman grave marker, the curious longing of Neruda's idolators: the wish for a stationary god, a known rather than an unknown god, a tractable god whose sources go docilely back to Whitman or Darío or Karl Marx—a fixed eminence pointing one way like the profiles of Easter Island toward the Chilean mainland: a mausoleum, a patriotic rubric for the good life, an irreversible Position. Precisely this is the measure of the anguish of Neruda's contradictory venture: to keep "empty," to test his *deberes*—the commitments of a lifetime—with imaginative acts of "non-being" forcing the poet to pit the personal against the political life; to invite trial by negation, reversal, suspension, self-doubt, in a hazardous insistence upon Muddlement: to be "rector of nothing" (*rector de nada*).

There is hardly any need, I think, to labor the obvious and painful conversion of Neruda by his Latin American admirers into a national acropolis and a gun emplacement for an ideological invasion. Nothing less elevated than the heights of Macchu Picchu will do. Neruda has recently protested in prose to a number of reporters whose questions were baited for more conventional outcomes. To *Le Monde*'s interviewer,[1] primarily concerned with the theme of multiple identities in *Estravagario,* he remarked: "When I was an exclusively introverted poet I was accused of being non-political. Then when I spoke out in behalf of man and man's suffering I was dragged off by the ears like a schoolboy and reprimanded by others. They have turned me into a shooting gallery." To an audience at the University of Chile he confided:[2]

> The poet is not a "little god"; he has not stolen celestial fire; he is not the offspring of a special race, androgynous or malign. He is a craftsman with a function. His function is no more important than other functions, except when he dares to confront the forces of social reaction. And that is dangerous too, because the poet speaks as a custodian of the truth.

He went on to elaborate to his Parisian interviewer:

> Every one of my poems is a little like a leap into the blue; I alternately jump out of the window onto the street, and back again through the window off of the street. I have always rejected a positional poetry (*poesía de especialista*) and shall always refuse to enclose myself in a single poetic modality (*un solo género poético*). After *Canto general,* it seemed to me I had exhausted the geo-historical concept of a poetry essentially preoccupied with the Latin American continent and ambience. Afterwards, I was threatened on all sides by purely pathetic incursions. I had to find a different tone, I had to *learn how to play* (*aprender a jugar*). I abandoned a terrorist or sanguinary poetry to write edible verses,

---

[1] Translated into Spanish for *Clarín literario* (Buenos Aires), October 28, 1971: *"La única ley del arte es vida,"* Aline Schulmann.

[2] From a review in *Clarín literario, ibid.: "La vida en versos,"* Uboldo Nicchi.

verses like treacle. I was straightway accused of being a programmatic optimist. I have never renounced my right to express the loneliness, the anguish, or the horror of things. My job is to capture the sounds, mingle the colors, probe for the vital power of things wherever they are to be found, by due process of creation and destruction.

Nevertheless, the myopic proscription of Neruda has gone on, and has recently been imported into this country by anthologists and translators by a kind of reverse imperialism which seeks to immobilize his diversity in "simplified" versions for the common reader. Robert Bly, for example, for all his raucous devotion to the genius of Neruda, has not only annexed him to the American Middle West, but finally bound him back-to-back with César Vallejo in a maudlin formula for the "open" way in poetry. Neruda took pains to point out the misdirection in an interview[3] with Mr. Bly, after courteously acknowledging his good intentions: "I like very much the way you approach us—that you bring us near each other in our work worlds. I never thought of it . . . Nevertheless we were very different. Race especially. He was Peruvian. He was a very Peruvian man—" by which, Neruda went on to specify, he meant that Vallejo was Indian. "I don't have it," he concluded categorically. "I am a Castillian poet. In Chile we defend the Indians and almost all South Americans have some Indian blood, I do too. But I don't think my work is in any way Indian."

Typical of the programmatic reduction of Neruda by Mr. Bly is the bristling choice of a title for his Introduction to an anthology of twenty poems loosely distributed over a period of twenty-nine years: "Refusing To Be Theocritus." The phrase itself, excerpted from a diffuse and journalistic poem

---

[3] *Twenty Poems* by Pablo Neruda. Translated by James Wright and Robert Bly. With Introduction and Interview by Robert Bly. The Sixties Press (Madison, Minnesota), 1967.

to the Venezuelan poet, Miguel Otero Silva, in effect equates the total accomplishment of Neruda with an episode in the '40's convenient for the purposes of Mr. Bly. His implied derogation of the pastoral way has a ring of evangelical ferocity. Theocritus, apparently, belongs with Watteau and Marie Antoinette—a perpetual fancy-dress ball in which shepherd-esses converse with shepherds twelve months of the year about love and scenery, and nothing ever changes but the seasons. In place of Theocritus, Bly has chosen to elevate an urban, unmetaphysical Neruda confronting the Secret Police of González Videla "with hands stained with depression and garbage"—and hold him to that tableau throughout the *Residencia en la tierra* (1925–1945), *Canto general* (1950), and the *Odas elementales* (1954–1959), like a panel in a post-office mural.

That is the *known* Neruda: the public klaxon or forensic convenience to which all roads have led with a shocking paucity of exceptions. Where exceptions exist, they have been the result of open-ended reading by inductive observers whose concern is with the momentum and idiosyncrasies of a total vision incorruptibly committed to its impulses. Thus it is that Neruda's discerning bibliographer at the University of Chile chose the motif of "Being and Dying"[4] as the riddle of the "moving finger" of Pablo Neruda; and the poet's Uruguayan biographer, in a more subtle reversal of that paradox, has traced the itinerary of an "Immobile Traveler."[5] The Neruda of both Hernán Loyola and Emir Rodríguez Monegal is seen not only face to face, but face after face. Each follows the contradictory voyage of a poet in its Lilliputian and Brobdingnagian phases without regard for equations of size or the protocol of the heroic stance. And, in fairness to Bly, it

---

[4] *Ser y morir en Pablo Neruda,* Hernán Loyola. Editorial Santiago (Santiago de Chile), 1967.

[5] *El viajero inmóvil.* Introducción a Pablo Neruda, Emir Rodríguez Monegal. Editorial Losada (Buenos Aires), 1966.

must be pointed out that even he sees somewhere in the middle distance a Neruda who "contains an astonishing variety of earthy things that swim in a sort of murky water," while opting for a "surrealist" activist.

And Neruda—what has he seen? Neruda's mistrust of his mentors—those presumably in the know, feeding an epoch's computers with cue cards for the mating of a poet with the politically nubile and lonely—has alternately plagued and amused him. His form of saying so has been odic—Theocritan:

> Came the critics: one deaf
> and one gifted with tongues,
> and others and others:
> the blind and the hundred-eyed,
> the elegant ones
> in red pumps and carnations,
> others decently clad
> like cadavers . . .
> some coiled in the forehead
> of Marx or thrashing about in his whiskers;
> others were English,
> just English . . .
>
> *(Oda a la crítica)*

In 1968 he was both truculent and fey:

> They keep after me
> with their questions: what are my relations
> with cats, how I discovered the rainbow,
> why the worth of the chestnut
> is contained in its burr . . .
> they want, of all things to know
> the bull-frog's opinion: what do
> animals under their burrows,
> in the fragrance of forests or
> in pustules of asphalt, make of my life?
>
> *(Abejas(I))*

Pablo Neruda / xix

With a marksman's eye for changing guards and vogues, he recently remarked to a startled reporter in Buenos Aires[6] (on a mission from the erudite *Razón y fábula* of Colombia's Universidad de los Andes):

> I assume that in a country (like Chile) that is going Socialist, the direction of poetry would have to be one of diversification, and that every poet would leave his own mark on the changing tradition. There must always be this diversity: that, precisely, is what insures the flowering of poetry under any circumstance. It's impossible to specify any one single road, poetry has many ways, every conceivable way . . . Poetry is always changing . . . The poets already known to us still write brilliant and interesting things, as they have in the past . . . In Chile (the Chile of Allende) poets have no intention of writing in any but their accustomed manner . . . We are about to nationalize a publishing house to serve the Chilean Republic—a colossal undertaking which has both its advantages and its possible risks.

Prodded by his questioner about "the future of poetry in a technological world," his reply was nothing short of ambassadorial:

> The jets breaking the sound barrier, and similar noises known to us all are altering the silence of the world. Poets are free to participate or not in the great hubbub of human progress on a technological level proper to such matters; but they must always keep sacrosanct some recess dedicated to their spiritual intimacy, to the task of self-knowledge, to the eternal experiment with words, sounds, and dreams.

---

[6] *"Pablo Neruda en Buenos Aires,"* Antonio Requieri, *Razón y fábula*, No. 24, marzo-avril, 1971.

For my own part, I have been influenced by all sorts of things in the exterior world, but I insist that nothing in the world that pressures us all with its gravity lessen my intimacy with myself. There's a verse of Whitman's that says: "Nothing exterior will ever command me completely."

Moving in closer, Neruda has constantly triangulated the stresses ("I remain steadfastly triangular") and jousted with faulting tastes and reputations in the aftermath of political eruptions. On occasion, would-be supplanters like Nicanor Parra have been named for him; at other times he has known where to plant the banderillas himself: Juan Larrea, or a whole *cuadrilla* of university *vallejistas* determined to undermine his prestige by the expropriation of a talent whose angle of vision has been repeatedly eulogized by Neruda in prose, verse, and personal interview: Peru's César Vallejo. Only two years ago, Neruda observed with characteristic taciturnity:

Those who were lately *nerudarized*
[*Todos los que nerudearon*]
are beginning to *vallejolate:*
[*comenzaron a vallejarse*]
before the cock crowed up the dawn
they settled for Eliot and Perse
and drowned in their fishpond.

Nevertheless I go on spinning
my own ancestral time-table,
chintzier with each passing day,
without discovering so much as a flower
not already discovered by others,
or inventing a single
fixed star not already extinct.

(*Ayer*)

Pablo Neruda / xxi

While others have been firing up their boilers like freight trains at Neruda's beloved old Mapocho station house for midnight runs to the border, Neruda has contemptuously rejected all schedules and itineraries of the *avant-garde*, including their technological fixation on a "new" poetry for all. Even his imagery has been tatterdemalion, quixotic:

> Next time I come back
> into time astride my habitual nag
> I'll give all my attention to stalking
> anything that moves—in the sky, on the ground,
> with the regulation hunterly crouch:
> that way, ahead of the game, I can check
> on what is or isn't invented already,
> discovered, or still undiscovered.
>
> (Ayer)

For Neruda in 1972, the rather seedy and categorical *mésalliance* of all Latin American modernism with Walt Whitman is still good enough, though he continues to press for the "Castillian" refinements of Góngora and Quevedo. His lapidary essay on Quevedo deserves to be better known, as well as the sumptuous Gongorism of certain sonnets and barcaroles, and those infiltrations (called "surrealist") that reverse the laconic journalism of lyric after lyric with seventeenth-century extravagances:

> Distance feeds on my clothing
> as I climb the titanic perspectives
>
> (Volver volviendo)

or a seascape:

> Convulsions, the tortoise's bitterness,
> a murderer's panoply,
> diapasons, wars to the death,
> a piano of slaughterer's teeth
>
> (Marejada en 1968: Océano Pacífico)

or the polarization of a crystal:

> the diamond's linear water: the maze
> in the sapphire and its gothic magnificence:
> the multiplication of rectangles
> in the nut of the amethyst . . .
> the salt's school; the decorum of fire.
>
>   (*El cuadrado al crystal*)

To this day, devotees of *Macchu Picchu* tend to forget that Section ix of that poem combines a Communist's metaphysics of rational faith with a counterplay of images which might tax the fantasy of a Gongorist, and merits Fernando Alegría's epithet of *"churrigueresco."*

Even the *"poetas celestes,"* the introspective pantheon of Rilke, Kafka, and Gide formerly denounced by Neruda as "obscurantists, false/existential witch doctors, surrealist/butterflies ablaze/on the carrion," have been recently assimilated into his oceanic tolerance as another part of the imaginative field. If Neruda is no longer a Theocritan, he is plainly Ovidian in his metamorphic passion for *change* as a mode of virility and a dynamic of cosmological love. He has changed not only from fat poems to skinny ones, or from open poems to orphic utterance; he has periodically changed the whole currency of his thinking—the mind of a man, as well as the mind of a poet—in a lifelong ventilation of commitments. Asked for his views regarding "the celestial poets" in 1966,[7] he replied disarmingly: "I must say I have been mistaken many times in my life. I was dogmatic and foolish . . . Excuse me, but the contradictions—one sees them only when life rolls on, one sees one has been mistaken." "Kafka is a great writer"; and more recently, Borges, who has not yet returned the compliment with comparable gusto, is "not only a great Argentine writer, but one of the most important in the entire world."[8] Rimbaud,

---

[7] *Twenty Poems, op. cit.*
[8] *Razón y fábula, op. cit.*

Emerson, Schiller, de Vigny, Hugo, Mallarmé, Apollinaire— the vegetal and the cerebral poets alike—have all been acknowledged as republican spirits in a tentative venture in which poets of all persuasions are indissolubly allied. "Who's to say whether one or the other approaches to poetry is the permanently viable one?"[9] This has not prevented him from changing his mind again in 1969 in another sweeping derogation of Verlaine, the "umbrellas of Baudelaire," the combined encumbrances of Balzac ("an elephant"), Hugo ("a truck"), Tolstoi ("a mountain"), Zola ("a cow"), and Mallarmé again ("a pastry-cook"), in favor of "Uncle Ubu Dada," who had the wit to say *merde* to them all.

Similarly, Neruda's revision of set-pieces variously entitled "The Poet," "Arte poética," or "Artes poéticas," over the years has been especially instructive and diverting, and continues into *World's End* (*Fin de mundo*, 1969) with two further variations on the theme. In *Residencia I* (1925–1931), for example, his inflection was one of plangent and harrowing melancholy, "between dark and the void . . . with my singular heart and my mournful conceits for my portion," and his poetics, a grinding ordeal of existential "absence" poised for a breakthrough which only the disaster of the Spanish Civil War could disclose to him:

> For every invisible drop that I taste in a stupor, alas,
> for each intonation I concentrate, shuddering,
> I keep the identical thrust of an absence, the identical
>   chill of a fever . . .
> Could it be differently put, a little less ruefully,
>   possibly?—
> All the truth blurted out?
>
> (Arte poética)

---

[9] *Razón y fábula, op. cit.*

In the end, he yielded to the pathos of the deracinated pre-
dicament and produced two other *Residencias* (1931–1935),
(1935–1945) in an

> impact of objects that call and encounter no answer,
> unrest without respite, the anomalous mind
> (*Arte poética*)

In *Canto general* (1950) the tone was more militant, though
still obsessively retrospective in its bid for a larger vision
hostile to the death-will and the limited life:

> That time when I moved among happenings
> in the midst of my mournful devotions . . .
> the inhuman
> contention of masks and existences.
> I endured in the bog-dweller's element . . .
> Estranged to myself, like shadow on water
> I sped through the exile of each man's existence
> this way and that, and so, to habitual loathing.
> (*El poeta*)

Here the conclusion may be called diagnostic or hermeneutic:
the physician, having learned how to heal himself, offers his
pharmacopeia to all:

> I saw that their being was this: to stifle
> one half of existence's fullness like fish
> in an alien margin of ocean.
> (*El poeta*)

By contrast, the poetics of *World's End* (1969) seem al-
most oafishly insouciant, unbuttoned, unforensic: a poetics
of vagary rather than the hard line of programmatic self-
criticism:

All really superior poets
laugh at my penmanship—
because of the punctuation—
while I keep thumping my breast
confessing my commas and periods,
colons, exclamation points:
all the incestuous and criminal
acts that have buried my words
in a Dark Ages special to me,
like provincial cathedrals.

(Ayer)

Of his two recent "Artes poéticas," the first, folksy and cerebral by turns, maintains a tone of garrulity and avoids the nomenclature common to the aesthetics of the imaginative process. Neruda puts on hat over hat over hat, with a clown's disregard for the gravity of alternative functions. He is carpenter-poet, "cutting into the board / of my choice / with the sputtering point of my saw"; a baker "wading in, to my elbows, / kneading the glare of the oven / into watery green language"/; and "blacksmith, perhaps," who requires "of myself and my verse . . . a metallurgical medium." Here his conclusion is to shrug off conclusion ("One poet's experience / with manual metaphysics / doesn't make a poetics"):

In this free confraternity
I've no burning allegiances.
I was always a lone iron-monger.

"Artes poéticas (II)" is even more spindly and wayward in its total disregard for the premise of the unprecedented vision—the Rimbaldian *voyant* or the Baudelairean *voyageur* pointing his prow toward infinity with a satanic insistence on the abyss of the Unexperienced, *"Enfer ou Ciel, qu'importe?"* For Neruda, the point for poetry is precisely the opposite: the enigmatic is what is totally given us, what is totally *there* —inexhaustible, inescapable, inapprehensible:

I've discovered nothing at all;
all was already discovered
when I ambled into the world.
If I come back this way
I entreat all discoverers
to leave something for me—
some unnamed volcano,
the secret source of a river,
an anonymous madrigal.

2

The point for the poetry of Pablo Neruda could also be a
wholly disastrous one. There will always be those who rise to
remark that I have been inadvertently notarizing the bank-
ruptcy and not the enrichment of a talent: that this is a cave-
in, a sell-out, the creeping liquidation of both a poet and a
political conscience. The "unknown Neruda" by this right
would be an eccentric and obsolescent Neruda—anti-intel-
lectual, chaplinesque, incorrigible: a poet without contour,
rigor, or direction. Such a mischievous reading of the record
would confirm again the old longing for a monolithic Neruda,
or the mandate for a permanent one—both inadmissible pro-
cedures in the critical appraisal of poets of genius anywhere
in the world.

That I have been noting an anti-heroic trend in the pos-
ture of the later Neruda, however, is a reading I would
happily affirm. The "unknown Neruda" must first be trans-
posed from Macchu Picchu—which, after all, is borrowed
tierra of distinctly Indian antiquity—to Isla Negra, which has
served for years as the bastion of a troubled Chilean turning
his vision outward and inward to answer the enigma of the
displaced identity in a "century of the stateless man": "What
can I do without roots?" The great poem of the "unknown

Neruda" is not "Las alturas de Macchu Picchu" but "Fin de fiesta" (Party's End) from the *Cantos ceremoniales* (1961)— a poem of haunting equivocations, with an "island music" as subtle as the watery and earthy noises caught in mid-air by the drunkards of *The Tempest*. As steward and enchanter of that island, Neruda, with wand and book, evokes the innocence of a "brave new world that hath such people in it," visions of shipwreck, dispossession, and the corrupt polity of the old world, while preparing a sea-change for a stranger reassertion of reality. For his attendant sprites he has both Ariel and Caliban; and behind them, the darker mythopoeia of Sycorax, the island's ambiguous progenetrix: daimons of earth, air, water, and fire, a supplanted and vaguely apotheosized mother, a "brusque father" buried "in one of the rainiest graveyards of the world," and an enigma directed variously at the human dream of liberty and the geology of the cosmos. All is in readiness, it would seem, for a Theocritan return to an idyl in the twentieth-century style—the metropolitan pastoral of the good society in which worker talks to worker twelve months of the year about love and the economics of abundance and nothing ever changes but the seasons.

It is precisely here, however, that the "unknown Neruda" intervenes, with a shocking reversal of protocol. What is likely to puzzle and mortify the partisan reader of *World's End* most is the unsparing embitterment of Neruda's castigation of a century, thirty years in advance of its legal and historical demise. Hernán Loyola[10] tells us that *Fin de mundo* originally bore the title of *Juicio final* (*Last Judgment*)—a wholly different conception from the kind of periodic stocktaking to which Neruda has shown an abiding partiality—last testaments, autumnal testaments, testimonials, witnesses, in the spirit of François Villon: "I am the sonorous man / wit-

[10] *Pablo Neruda: Antología esencial. Selección y prólogo de Hernán Loyola,* Editorial Losada (Buenos Aires), 1971.

ness [*testigo*] to the hopes of this murderous century." An overlay of all these titles—*Fin de fiesta, Fin de mundo, Juicio final*—reveals the eschatological passion with which Neruda, writing as though every book was his last, since *Canto general*, and signing his vision of judgment with his flayed skin, like Michelangelo, has finally aggrandized his dream of the human condition:

> I wait at this door
> for those still to come to this party's end:
> to this end of the world.
>
> (*La puerta*)

The roll call of despairing epithets applied to his century in *World's End* is literally annihilating: one would have to go back to Jeremiah or to *The Wasteland* to equal it. "This is the hollow century," "This is the epoch of ashes," "This is the century of agony / that taught us how to kill / and to die like survivors," "This century swarming / with rightists and leftists / robbers of man, usurpers / kidnappers, murderers," the "electronic century" of a "new god with an eye in its forehead / to kill us," "the century of the displaced man / the book of displacement / the dark century, the black book / given me to write and hold to the light," etc., etc. Indeed, it would seem that Neruda's "book of displacement" is even more lethal than he may have bargained for: Timon of Athens has moved into the island kingdom of Prospero and reigns as tyrant of a malevolent century:

> we hear not only the knife
> cutting the sky
> and dividing the planets,
> but in damnable islands the poets
> of Athens still live in chains.
>
> (*Siglo*)
>
> *Pablo Neruda* / **xxix**

The truth is: I never understood
anyone's messages . . .
Only the Ocean existed.

(*El mar*)

I have lived one hundred years
moving from one war to the next
drinking blood out of books,
out of newspapers and
television, at home
on trains, in the Spring,
in my mourning for Spain.

(*Vivir cien años*)

The truth is that there is no truth.

(*Exilios*)

This, too, is an unknown Neruda—the most misanthropic
given us since his purgatorial voyage through three *Residen-
cias*—a Neruda to be reckoned with, as one reckons with the
contrary states of innocence and experience of the Mental
Traveler (a poem translated by Neruda in 1934) in Blake's
similar search for revolutionary "progression." For revolution
and progression are there: they are the inalienable act of
faith in a long discipline of "*deberes*"—the heart as well as the
conscience of Neruda's poetics of "obligation." What has
apparently withered away is the dialectical optimism of a
Marxist reading of history. While others have turned to "the
hypothetical politician / who leads without leadership / in-
visible multitudes," Neruda has remained a "lone iron-mon-
ger"—a type of the simultaneous man ordering the chaos of
poetry by spontaneous enactments of being, rather than a
timetable for the withering away of the dictatorship by the
proletariat. As of 1972, *all* is equally "impure" for Neruda:
poetry, history, destiny, the hope of the world, while a poet
who has "learned how to *play*" with fatality as well as envi-

sion and indict it, "plays with the darkness / without forget-
ting the good days."

It is in "games" as vast and portentous as this that the ten-
sions of *The Hands of Day, World's End,* and *The Stones of
the Sky* (*Piedras del cielo:* 1970) must be realigned to engage
the full magnitude of the unknown Neruda. The "games" are
the games which poets of multinational genius have always
played, to the exasperation of philosopher kings and theoreti-
cal utopists: the games by which we recognize the truly
laureate poet, who comes to say in the end that "Hamlet and
Lear are gay." It is not idle perversity that induces Neruda to
write in the twilight of an obsessional "song of myself":

> Condemned to self-love,
> I lived the exterior life of a hypocrite
> hiding the depths of the love
> my defects brought down on my head.
> I keep on being happy,
> disclosing to nobody
> my ambiguous malady:
> the grief I endure for self-love,
> who was never so loved in return.
>
> (*Condiciones*)

and to add:

> The harsher the street sounds became,
> the sweeter I seemed to myself.

The "happiness" of Neruda is apparent throughout each of
the three volumes excerpted for this collection: it is the
"ounce of civet" with which an offended imagination has been
sweetened in antic and diminished acts of lyricism. The tone
is not euphoric or rational, but vitalistic and disengaged; and
the sweetness is the sweetness of a whole organism soundly
fulfilling its visceral and intellectual life functions. Neruda

is neither eclectic, nor ambivalent, nor contradictory in the sense that one has reason to anticipate a synthesis that never materializes: he is as multiple as he needs to be. There is room even for Theocritus: he returns as "root-hunter" (*cazador de raíces*) and interpreter of rains and volcanoes in the *Memorial de Isla Negra* (1964), writing landscape after landscape, attempting a paganization of the myth of Genesis in *The Burning Sword* (*La espada encendida:* 1970), and finally turning the Pacific itself into a pasture of plankton for narwhals and leviathans. The uncanny light of that serenity is the mark of the "unknown Neruda" as the light of Velásquez is the signature of the later Velásquez. It shows us Neruda at his games and *deberes,* indicting a century, "playing" with the cyclical notion of a century of "hands" (more "manual metaphysics!") in *The Hands of Day,* and transmuting the *Stones of Chile* (*Las piedras de Chile:* 1961)—the rocky crenellations of his island fortress of Isla Negra—into geological transparencies. In 1970, whatever is hardest, least diaphanous and destructible, most geometrical in the vision of Pablo Neruda has turned into a crystal fitting for a sibyl: "the stones of the sky."

—Ben Belitt

Bennington College
Bennington, Vermont

I: *Las manos del día* / The Hands of Day
(1968)

ENIGMA CON UNA FLOR

Una victoria. Es tarde, no sabías.
Llegó como azucena a mi albedrío
el blanco talle que traspasa
la eternidad inmóvil de la tierra,
empujando una débil forma clara
hasta horadar la arcilla
con rayo blanco o espolón de leche.
Muda, compacta oscuridad del suelo
en cuyo precipicio
avanza la flor clara
hasta que el pabellón de su blancura
derrota el fondo indigno de la noche
y de la claridad en movimiento
se derraman atónitas semillas.

ENIGMA WITH A FLOWER

Victory. It is later than you knew.
The white stalk that transfixes
earth's unmoving eternity
rose to my need like a lily,
pushing a frail, clear form
till it struck through the clay
in a breakwater of milk, a white scintillation.
In the dark of the soil, mute and compact,
in the precipice,
the clear flower advanced
till whiteness was all, a pavilion
breaking night's abject abysses,
and in the moved incandescence
the seeds spilled over, amazed.

OTROS DIOSES

Los dioses blancos duermen
en los libros:
se les ha roto el almidón, el frío
les devoró los ojos,
subsisten sin la claridad de entonces
y apenas queda una memoria
de amor entre los muslos.

La estatua quebrada
no guardó en la cintura
los relámpagos.

Se apagó la blancura.

Sin embargo, sabed, héroes cansados,
de rodillas de mármol,
que el dios intransigente
de las islas marinas
o la hirsuta, emplumada,
sangrienta
divinidad del África,
ceñuda en su envoltorio
o desnuda en la fiesta de la especie,
fiera tribal o corazón totémico,
tambor, escudo, lanza que vivió en la espesura
o junto a negros ríos que lloraban,
siguen ardiendo, vivos,
actuales, ancestrales,
llenos de sangre y sueños y sonidos:
aún no se sentaron en el trono
como espectros de mármol
nacidos de la espuma,
sino que continúan en la sombra
su sombría batalla.

OTHER GODS

The white gods sleep
in the books:
time broke their starches, cold
gnawed at their eyes,
they outlived the old clarities
with hardly a passion
their thighs can remember.

Their waists of wrecked plaster
no longer keep
the old rage.

The white has blown out.

Tired heroes,
brought to your knees in white marble, know
once and for all, the intransigent god
of the watery islands,
the African godhead,
hairy, bloody,
and plumed,
encumbered like bundles
or nude in the feasts of the species,
the beasts of the tribe, the totemical heart,
drum, shield, lance that thrives on the grossness of things
or by mourning black rivers,
go on living and burning,
alive and ancestral,
full of visions and noises and blood,
not throned
like those figments of marble
struck out of spray,
but unwearied still in the dark
and the battles of darkness.

EL CAMPANERO

Aun aquel que volvió
del monte, de la arena,
del mar, del mineral, del agua,
con las manos vacías,
aun el domador
que volvió del caballo
en un cajón, quebrado
y fallecido
o la mujer de siete manos
que en el telar
perdió de pronto el hilo
y regresó al ovario,
a no ser más que harapo,
o aun el campanero
que al mover
en la cuerda
el firmamento
cayó de las iglesias
hacia la oscuridad
y el cementerio:
aun todos ellos
se fueron
con las manos gastadas
no por la suavidad sino por algo:
el tiempo corrosivo,
la substancia
enemiga
del carbón, de la ola,
del algodón, del viento,
porque sólo el dolor enseñó a ser:
porque hacer fue el destino de las manos
y en cada cicatriz cabe la vida.

THE BELL-RINGER

Even the mountaineer came back
from the mountain, from sand,
sea, the mineral world, water,
empty-handed;
the breaker of horses came back
unhorsed,
broken by death
in a box;
and the seven-handed woman
suddenly fumbled the thread
in the loom
and went back to the womb,
no more than a rag;
even the bell-ringer
moving
the sky
on a cord,
fell from the church
through the dark
of the graveyard;
even these
went away
with hands worn
by no burnish but some other unspeakable thing:
corrosive time.
the inimical
substance
of coal, waves,
cotton, wind:
because grief taught us to be,
because the hands' work is a destiny
and life shapes itself to their scars.

LA MANO CENTRAL

Tocar la acción, vivir la transparencia
del cristal en el fuego,
circular en el bronce
hasta cantar por boca de campana,
olorosa alegría
de la tabla que gime
como un violín
en el aserradero,
polvo del pan
que viaja
desde una rumorosa
conversación de espigas
hasta la máquina
de los panaderos,
tocar la desventura
del carbón
en su muerta catarata
sometido al latido
de las excavaciones
hasta quebrarse, huir,
aliarse y revivir
en el acero
tomando la unidad
de la pureza, la paloma ovalada
del nuevo movimiento:
acción,
acción de sangre:
circulación del fuego:
circuito de las manos:
rosa de la energía.

THE CENTRAL HAND

To touch action: live out the fire
of the crystal's transparency,
to whirl in the bronze
till the bell mouth sings out;
the fragrant delight
of the board that whines
like a fiddlestring
under the saw,
pollen of bread
that sails
from the whispered
exchange of the wheat
to the baker's machinery;
to touch the disaster
of coal,
a cataract stopped
by the pulse
of the drillers,
wrecked, cast-off,
reassembled, revived
in an ingot of steel
taking the wholeness of things,
perfection, the dove's ovalling
motion renewed:
action,
blood's act:
the fire's circulation:
the hand's circuit:
energy's rose.

Pablo Neruda / 9

SEMEN

Porque ese grito no tiene palabra
es sólo sílaba color de sangre.

Y circula en el giro de un deseo
como un espeso manantial caliente:
sulfato de cal roja, sol secreto
que abre y cierra las puertas genitales.

SEMEN

Because no words suffice for this cry
it lives as a blood-colored syllable.

And circles a ring of desire
like a cloudburst, sultry and dense:
red sulphate of quicklime, a secret sun
opening and closing the genital doors.

CASA DE MANTARAS EN PUNTA DEL ESTE

Cuántas cosas caen del pino,
bigotes verdes,
música,
piñas como peñascos
o armadillos
o como libros para deshojar.

También cayó en mi cara
el pétalo sutil
que sujetaba una semilla negra:
era un ala himenóptera
del pino,
una transmigración
de suavidades
en que el vuelo se unía
a las raíces.

Caen
gotas del árbol,
puntuaciones,
vocales, consonantes,
violines,
cae lluvia,
silencio,
todo cae del pino,
del aire vertical:
cae el aroma,
la sombra acribillada
por el día,
la noche clara
como leche de luna,

CASA DE MANTARAS EN PUNTA DEL ESTE

Strange things fall from the pine,
green mustaches,
music,
peaked pinecones,
armadillos,
torn leaves of a book.

So, too, on my face
the delicate petal
guided a fall of black seed:
it was a hymenopterous wing
of the pine,
a transmigration of
glosses
whose flight
was one with its roots.

Drops fall
from the tree,
punctuation,
consonants, vowels,
violins,
rain falls
and silence,
all falls from the pine
through the vertical air:
aromas fall,
shadows pierced
by the day,
lunar milk
of night's clarity,

la noche negra
como aquella ausencia.

Amanece.

Y cae
un nuevo día
desde lo alto del pino,
cae con su reloj,
con sus agujas
y sus agujeros,
y anocheciendo cosen
las agujas del pino
otra noche a la luz,
otro día a la noche.

night black
with its absence.

It begins to grow light.

A new day
falls
from the height of the pine,
falls with its clocks
and its pointers,
its pot-holes;
and turning again to the dark, it stitches
with needles of pine
another night to the light
another day to the night.

YO NO SÉ NADA

En el perímetro y la exactitud
de ciencias inexactas, aquí estoy, compañeros,
sin saber explicar estos vocablos
que se trasladan poco a poco al cielo
y que prueban robustas existencias.

De nada nos valió
hundir el avestruz en la cabeza,
o hacernos agujeros en la tierra,
"No hay nada que saber, se sabe todo."
"No nos molesten con la geometría."

Lo cierto es que una abstracta incertidumbre
sale de cada caos que regresa
cada vez a ser orden,
y qué curioso, todo
comienza con palabras,
nuevas palabras que se sientan solas
a la mesa, sin previa invitación,
palabras detestables que tragamos
y que se meten en nuestros armarios,
en nuestras camas, en nuestros amores,
hasta que son: hasta que comienza
otra vez el comienzo por el verbo.

I KNOW NOTHING AT ALL

In the perimeter and exactitude
of the inexact sciences, there you have me, my
    friends,
not knowing how to explain all those vocables
that move toward the sky, little by little,
to robuster existences.

We get nothing
by knocking the ostrich's head
and making our hole in the ground.
"Everyone knows that there's nothing to know."
"Don't rattle our brains with geometry."

This much is sure: an abstract uncertainty
comes and goes with each chaos, to turn
into order again;
and oddly enough, all
starts with a word,
new words that sit themselves down
detestable words we toss off,
at the table, alone, uninvited,
that rummage our clothes closets,
get into our beds and our loves,
and stay on for good: till
the beginning begins once again with a word.

UN ESCARABAJO

También llegué al escarabajo
y le pregunté por la vida:
por sus costumbres en otoño,
por su armadura lineal.

Lo busqué en los lagos perdidos
en el Sur negro de mi patria,
lo encontré entre la ceniza
de los volcanes rencorosos
o subiendo de las raíces
hacia su propia oscuridad.

Cómo hiciste tu traje duro?
Tus ojos de zinc, tu corbata?
Tus pantalones de metal?
Tus contradictorias tijeras?
Tu sierra de oro, tus tenazas?
Con qué resina maduró
la incandescencia de tu especie?

(Yo hubiera querido tener
un corazón de escarabajo
para perforar la espesura
y dejar mi firma escondida
en la muerte de la madera.)
((Y así mi nombre alguna vez
de nuevo irá tal vez naciendo
por nuevos canales nocturnos
hasta salir por fin del túnel
con otras alas venideras.))

((Nada más hermoso que tú
mudo, insondable escarabajo,

BEETLE

I went to the beetle
with my question about life:
the rites of his autumn,
his linear armor.

I hunted him down in the lost lakes
of the black south of my country.
I found him in the volcano's
malevolent ash,
or followed the fall of his roots
into innermost darkness.

How did you work those hard things?
Your zinc eyes and your necktie?
Your cast-iron trousers?
Your contradictory scissors?
Your gold ridges, the tongs of your claws?
What resins could ripen
the incandescence of your kind?

For myself I ask only
a scarab's heart
to push past the densities
and sign my name's secret
in the death of the wood.
(Who knows? My name might take on
new life, turn to the light
new channels in midnight,
come out at the opposite end of the tunnel
with the other wings waiting their turn?)

What is prettier than you,
beetle, inscrutably mute,

sacerdote de las raíces,
rinoceronte del rocío,))
le dije, pero no me dijo.

Le pregunté y no contestó.

Así son los escarabajos.

priest of the roots,
rhinoceros of dew,
I said. He said nothing.

I asked. He said nothing.

There's a beetle for you.

EL ENFERMO TOMA EL SOL

Qué haces tú, casi muerto, si el nuevo día Lunes
hilado por el sol, fragante a beso,
se cuelga de su cielo señalado
y se dedica a molestar tu crisis?

Tú ibas saliendo de tu enfermedad,
de tus suposiciones lacerantes
en cuyo extremo el túnel
sin salida, la oscuridad con su final dictamen
te esperaba: el silencio
del corazón o de otra
víscera amenazada
te hundió en la certidumbre del adiós
y cerraste los ojos, entregado
al dolor, a su viento sucesivo.

Y hoy que desamarrado de la cama
ves tanta luz que no cabe en el aire
piensas que si, que si te hubieras muerto
no sólo no hubiera pasado nada
sino que nunca cupo tanta fiesta
como en el bello día de tu entierro.

SICK MAN IN THE SUN

What would it profit you, now as good as dead, if
   Monday came
round again, ripe as a kiss, woven with sun,
loosened its place in the sky
and aimed its full force at your worsening crisis?

You rose in your illness
and the bitter foreknowledge
at whose end the impassable
tunnel, dark with its final proscriptions,
awaits you: your heart's
silence, or some other
visceral menace
that hurts with its certain farewells;
your eyes closed, you delivered yourself
to your pain, gust after gust, like a wind.

Today, disinterred from your bed,
you see such unboundable light in the air
and you think: yes, should you die on such a day,
not only would nothing have happened,
but no festival would ever have equalled
the measure of this one, the heyday of your burial.

ARRABALES (CANCIÓN TRISTE)

Andando por San Antonio arriba
vi la quietud de la pobreza:
rechinaban los goznes quebrados,
las puertas cansadas querían
ir a sollozar o a dormir.
Debajo de los cristales rotos
en las ventanas, alguna flor,
un geranio amargo y sediento,
sacaba a pasear por la calle
su anaranjado fuego sucio.

Los niños del silencio aquel
desde sus ojos negros me vieron
como mirando desde un pozo,
desde las aguas olvidadas.

De pronto entró por la calle el viento
como si buscara su casa.
Se movieron los papeles muertos,
el polvo, perezosamente,
cambió de sitio, se agitó
un trapo en la ventana rota
y todo siguió como estaba:
la calle inmóvil, los ojos
que me miraron desde el pozo,
las casas que no parecían
esperar a nadie, las puertas
ya demolidas y desnudas:
todo era duro y polvoriento:
estaba muerto, estaba vivo,
quería morir y nacer.

Se preparaba para el fuego
la madera de la pobreza.

ARRABALES (SAD SONG)

Walking up San Antonio
I saw the quiet way of the poor:
broken hinges that rasped,
tired doors wanting only
to sob or to sleep.
Under smashed window-glass
some flowers on a windowsill,
a bitter and thirsty geranium,
took off down the street
in a fire's dirty orange.

The children of silence, looking
out of black eyes saw me go by,
as if from the depths of a well
and the water's stagnation.

A breeze suddenly entered the street
as if asking the way home.
Dead papers fluttered,
the dust dangerously
shifted position, rattled
a rag in the rubbish of windows,
and all went on as before:
the motionless street, the eyes
looking for me from their well,
the house seeming to expect
nobody at all, the doors
still demolished and naked:
all was dusty and obdurate,
dead, but alive,
all wanted to die or be born.

The wood of the poor
was preparing itself for the fire.

LA SOMBRA

Aún no vuelvo,
no he vuelto,
ando de viaje adentro
de la conflagración:
adentro de esta
vena
siguió viaje la sangre
y no puedo llegar
adentro de mí mismo.

Veo las plantas, las personas vivas,
las ramas del recuerdo,
el saludo en los ojos de las cosas,
la cola de mi perro.
Veo el silencio de mi casa, abierto
a mi voz, y no rompo las paredes
con un grito de piedra o de pistola:
ando por terreno que conoce mis pies,
toco la enredadera que subió
por los arcos oscuros de granito
y resbalo en las cosas,
en el aire,
porque sigue mi sombra en otra parte
o soy la sombra de un porfiado ausente.

SHADOW

I who shall never come back
and have never returned
continue my journey
inside the holocaust:
though the blood
races on
through my veins
I shall never arrive
at my selfhood within.

I see plants, living presences,
I remember branches,
all things salute me, I am seen
by the tail of my dog.
The peace of my house is alive
with my voice: I take care not to bring
the walls down with the cry of a rock or a pistol:
I walk on a soil that remembers my footsteps,
touch vines in the dark
climbing archways of granite—
but somewhere I slip, I lose
footing in mid-air
on the things of the world:
somewhere, in some part of myself, I am stalked by my
    shadow;
or turn into a shadow myself, the absent and obstinate
    one.

EL CANTO

La mano en la palabra,
la mano en medio
de lo que llamaban Dios,
la mano en la medida,
en la cintura del alma.

Hay que alarmar las cajas del idioma,
sobresaltar hasta que vuelen
como gaviotas las vocales,
hay que amasar
el barro
hasta que cante,
ensuciarlo con lágrimas,
lavarlo con sangre,
teñirlo con violetas
hasta que salga el río,
todo el río,
de una pequeña vasija:
es el canto:
la palabra
del río.

SONG

The hand on the word,
the hand in the midst
of the word for a God,
the hand on the measuring span,
on the waist of our spirits.

We must shake up the box of our language,
startle the vocables
till they circle like seagulls;
we must pound out
the mud like a batter
till it sings;
all must be soiled with our tears,
washed with our blood,
all take the violet's tint
till a river leaps forth,
the whole of a river
in the span of a tea-cup;
so goes the song:
that is the word
for a river.

EL REGALO

De cuántas duras manos
desciende la herramienta,
la copa,
y hasta la curva insigne
de la cadera que persigue luego
a toda la mujer con su dibujo!

Es la mano que forma
la copa de la forma,
conduce el embarazo del tonel
y la línea lunar de la campana.

Pido unas manos grandes
que me ayuden
a cambiar el perfil de los planetas:
estrellas triangulares
necesita el viajero:
constelaciones como dados fríos
de claridad cuadrada:
unas manos que extraigan
ríos secretos para Antofagasta
hasta que el agua rectifique
su avaricia perdida en el desierto.

Quiero todas las manos de los hombres
para amasar montañas
de pan y recoger
del mar todos los peces,
todas las aceitunas
del olivo,
todo el amor que no despierta aún
y dejar un regalo
en cada una de las manos
del día.

THE GIFT

From what hardened hands
the tool comes to us,
and the cup,
the notable curve
of a hip that clings to
the whole of a woman and prints itself there!

Hands shaping
the cup to its contour,
showing the way to the barrel's rotundity,
the lunar outline of the bell.

I need big hands
to help me
change the profile of planets;
the traveler requires
triangular stars;
constellations like dice
cut into squares by the cold;
hands that distill
hidden rivers in Antofagasta
and restore to the water
what its avarice lost in the desert.

I want all the hands of the world
to knead mountains
of bread, gather
all fish in the sea,
all the fruit
of the olive,
all the love still unawakened,
and leave
gifts
in the hands
of the day.

A SENTARSE

Todo el mundo sentado
a la mesa,
en el trono,
en la asamblea,
en el vagón del tren,
en la capilla,
en el océano,
en el avión, en la escuela, en el estadio
todo el mundo sentados o sentándose:
pero no habrá recuerdo
de una silla
que hayan hecho mis manos.

Qué pasó? Por qué, si mi destino
me llevó a estar sentado, entre otras cosas,
por qué no me dejaron
implantar cuatro patas
de un árbol extinguido
al asiento, al respaldo,
a la persona próxima
que allí debió aguardar el nacimiento
o la muerte de alguna que él amaba?
(La silla que no pude, que no hice,
transformando en estilo
la naturalidad de la madera
y en aparato claro
el rito de los árboles sombríos.)

La sierra circular
como un planeta
descendió de la noche
hasta la tierra.

SITTING DOWN

The whole world seated
at table,
on thrones,
in assemblies,
in railway compartments,
in chapels
and oceans,
airplanes, stadia, schools,
a whole world sitting down, or prepared to sit down—
yet no one will ever have reason
to remember a chair
that I made with my hands.

What happened? Why, if my lot
was (among other things) to be seated,
was I never allowed
to fit the four wasted paws
of a tree
to the seat of a chair or the rungs of its back
for the next man
to sweat out the birth
or the death of the woman he loved?
(The chair I could never imagine or build for myself,
transforming wood's properties
into an attitude,
the shadowy rites of a tree
to a lucid commodity?)

A circular saw
came down and touched earth
in the night,
like a planet.

Pablo Neruda / 33

Y rodó por los montes
de mi patria,
pasó sin ver por mi puerta larvaria,
se perdió en su sonido.
Y así fue como anduve
en el aroma
de la selva sagrada
sin agredir con hacha la arboleda,
sin tomar en mis manos
la decisión y la sabiduría
de cortar el ramaje
y extraer
una silla
de la inmovilidad
y repetirla
hasta que esté sentado todo el mundo.

It circled the peaks
of my country,
passed with no thought for the larvae at work in my door,
and was lost in a sound.
Since then, I have walked
through the smells
of the forest, holding everything sacred,
never slashing a tree with a hatchet,
never forcing
the wit or the will of my hands
to cut through the branches
and retrieve
from the stillness of things
one chair,
repeating it over and over
till there were chairs enough for a world and everyone sat
   down.

UNA CASA

Alguien toca una piedra y luego estalla
la piedra y los pedazos
se amalgaman de nuevo:
es la tarea
de los jóvenes dioses espulsados
del jardín solitario.
Es la tarea de
romper, restablecer,
quebrar, pegar, vencer
hasta que aquella roca
obedeció a las manos de Aguilera,
a los ojos de Antonio y Recaredo,
a la cabeza de don Alejandro.

Así se hacen las casas en la costa.

Y luego entran y salen las pisadas.

A HOUSE

Someone touches a stone, the stone
flies apart, the pieces
are fitted together again:
so the gods in their youth
cast out of gardens
might have toiled in their solitude.
Their labor:
to smash and restore,
to splinter and pound, overcome
all that was rock
till it yields to the hand of Aguilera,
the eyes of Antonio, Recaredo,
the head of don Alejandro.

That's how we build in the coastland.

Then, the coming and going of footsteps.

Es esta el alma suave que esperaba,
esta es el alma de hoy, sin movimiento,
como si estuviera hecha de luna
sin aire, quieta en su bondad terrible.

Cuando caiga una piedra
como un puño
del cielo de la noche
en esta copa la recibiré:
en la luz rebosante
recibiré la oscuridad viajera,
la incertidumbre celeste.

No robaré sino este movimiento
de la hierba del cielo,
de la noche fértil:
sólo un golpe de fuego,
una caída.

Líbrame, tierra oscura, de mis llaves:
si pude abrir y refrenar
y volver a cerrar el cielo duro,
doy testimonio de que no fui nada,
de que no fui nadie,
de que no fui.

Solo esperé la estrella,
el dardo de la luna,
el rayo de piedra celeste,
esperé inmóvil en la sociedad
de la hierba que crece en primavera,
de la leche en la ubre,
de la miel perezosa y peregrina:
esperé la esperanza,

Here's the amenable spirit I hoped for:
here, the soul of a day, made immobile
like a piece of the moon
strangled and stilled in its terrible charity.

A stone falls at night
like a fist
from the sky
and I catch it here in this cup:
I hold the wandering dark,
the celestial uncertainty,
in the light that brims over.

All I want is a tremor of
heavenly grass,
the nighttime's fertility,
thief of a fiery blow
and a fall.

Dark earth, deliver me of my keys:
if I could open the obstinate sky, subdue it,
and close it again,
I could prove I was nothing,
I am nobody,
I never existed at all.

I watched for a star,
an arrowhead in the moon,
a ray of sidereal stone,
without stirring a limb I waited
in the grass's society that feeds
on the milk in the udder,
the errant and indolent honey of spring:
I awaited the hope of a world

Pablo Neruda / 39

y aquí estoy
convicto
de haber pactado con la tempestad,
de haber aceptado la ira,
de haber abierto el alma,
de haber oído entrar al asesino,
mientras yo conversaba con la noche.

Ahí viene otro, dijo ladrando el perro.

Y yo con mis ojos de frío,
con el luto plateado
que me dio el firmamento,
no vi el puñal ni el perro,
no escuché los ladridos.

Y aquí estoy cuando nacen las semillas
y se abren como labios:
todo es fresco y profundo.

Estoy muerto,
estoy asesinado:
estoy naciendo
con la primavera.

Aquí tengo una hoja,
una oreja, un susurro,
un pensamiento:
voy a vivir otra vez,
me duelen las raíces,
el pelo,
me sonríe la boca:
me levanto
porque ha salido el sol.

Porque ha salido el sol.

and am culpable
now:
I have conspired with the tempest,
consented to anger,
laid open my soul,
I have heard the murderer enter
while I talked with the night.

Here comes another one, as the dog said, with a bark.

With frost in my eyes,
the silver and sackcloth
given to me by the sky,
I saw neither the dagger's blow nor the dog,
I heard nobody barking.

Now I watch seeds
breaking open, parting like mouths.
All is fresh and ineffable.

I am dead.
I am murdered.
I am coming to life
in the spring.

Here's a leaf,
here, an ear, a sigh,
a perception:
I am coming to life again.
I ache to the roots
of my hair,
my mouth opens out in a smile:
I get up
because the sun has gone out of the sky.

Because the sun has gone out of the sky.

EL GOLPE

Tinta que me entretienes
gota a gota
y vas guardando el rastro
de mi razón y de mi sinrazón
como una larga cicatriz que apenas
se verá, cuando el cuerpo esté dormido
en el discurso de sus destrucciones.

Tal vez mejor hubiera
volcado en una copa
toda tu esencia, y haberla arrojado
en una sola página, manchándola
con una sola estrella verde
y que sólo esa mancha
hubiera sido todo
lo que escribí a lo largo de mi vida,
sin alfabeto ni interpretaciones:
un solo golpe oscuro
sin palabras.

THE BLOW

Ink that enchants me,
drop after drop,
guarding the path
of my reason and unreason
like the hardly visible
scar on a wound that shows while the body sleeps
on in the discourse of its destructions.

Better
if the whole of your essence erupted
in a drop, to
vent itself on a page, staining it now
with a single green star;
better, perhaps, if that blot
gathered
my whole scribbling lifetime
without glosses or alphabets:
a single dark blow
without words.

II: *Fin de mundo* / World's End
(1969)

EL MISMO

Me costó mucho envejecer,
acaricié la primavera
como a un mueble recién comprado,
de madera olorosa y lisa,
y en sus cajones escondidos
acumulé la miel salvaje.

Por eso sonó la campana
llevándose a todos los muertos
sin que la oyera mi razón:
uno se acostumbra a su piel,
a su nariz, a su hermosura,
hasta que de tantos veranos
se muere el sol en su brasero.

Mirando el saludo del mar
o su insistencia en el tormento
me quedé volando en la orilla
o sentado sobre las olas
y guardo de este aprendizaje
un aroma verde y amargo
que acompaña mis movimientos.

THE SAME

It costs much to grow old:
I've fondled the Springs
like sticks of new furniture
with the wood still sweet to the smell, suave
in the grain, and hidden away in its lockers,
I've stored my wild honey.

That's why the bell tolled
bearing its sound to the dead,
out of range of my reason:
one grows used to one's skin,
the cut of one's nose, one's good looks,
while summer by summer, the sun
sinks in its brazier.

Noting the sea's health,
its insistence on turbulence,
I kept skimming the beaches;
now seated on waves
I keep the bitter green smell
of a lifetime's apprenticeship
to live on in the whole of my motion.

EL FUEGO

Qué momento tan musical
me dice un río inteligente
al mover junto a mí sus aguas:
él se divierte con las piedras,
sigue cantando su camino,
mientras yo decidido a todo
lo miro con ojos de furia.

Dediquemos a la desdicha
un pensamiento vaporoso
como la tierra matinal
sucia de lágrimas celestes
levanta un árbol de vapor
que desenfoca la mañana:
sufre la luz que iba naciendo,
se amotina la soledad
y ya no se cuenta con nada,
no se ve el cielo ni la tierra
bajo la neblina salobre.

Exageramos este asunto
dije volviendo a la fogata
que se apagaba en la espesura
y con dos ramas de laurel
se levantó una llama roja
con una castaña en el centro,
y luego se abrió la castaña
enseñándome la lección
de su dulzura aprisionada
y volví a ser un ciudadano
que quiere leer los periódicos.

THE FIRE

What a musical moment,
the intelligent river tells me,
moving close with its waters:
it amuses itself with its stones,
keeps its path singing
while I settle my jaw once
and for all, and watch with cold fury.

Let's keep one nebulous
thought for the malcontent,
as the world every morning,
transcendental and grimy with tears,
holds one great tree of air
that dislimns all the daylight:
light suffers itself to be born,
solitude mutinies,
till nothing remains to be seen,
neither sky nor the earth,
in the mist and brine of the distance.

But we exaggerate, I
said, looking back at the bonfires
that sank in the density:
two branches of laurel
and a red flame arose out of nowhere,
with a chestnut tree in the center:
then the tree itself opened out,
bearing tidings, the reminder
of sweetness imprisoned—
so I went back to my newspaper
and read on, like any good citizen.

HOY ES TAMBIÉN

Florece este día de invierno
con una sola rosa muerta,
la noche prepara su nave
caen los pétalos del cielo
y sin rumbo vuelve la vida
a recogerse en una copa.

Yo no sé decir de otro modo:
la noche negra, el día rojo,
y recibo las estaciones
con cortesía de poeta:
espero puntual la llegada
de las verbales golondrinas
y monto una guardia de acero
frente a las puertas del otoño.

Por eso el invierno imprevisto
me sobrecoge en su accidente
como el humo desalentado
del recuerdo de una batalla:
no es la palabra *padecer*,
no es *escarmiento,* no es *desdicha,*
es como un sonido en la selva,
como un tambor bajo la lluvia.
Lo cierto es que cambia mi tema
con el color de la mañana.

TODAY TOO

The winter's day blossoms
like one withered rose,
night readies its ship,
petals drop from the sky,
life returns, going nowhere,
to gather itself in a cup.

I can't say it otherwise:
black night, red day,
I receive all the seasons
with a poet's decorum:
I await the timely arrival
of talkative swallows
and keep steely watch
on the doorways of autumn.

That's why winter surprised me,
unforeseen, with its air of an accident,
like the smoky exhaust
of a battle remembered:
to suffer; punishment; hard luck—
those aren't the words for it.
It's more like a sound in a jungle,
a drumskin under the rain.
My theme changes with the color
of morning: only that much is certain.

SIEMPRE NACER

El sol nace de su semilla
a su esplendor obligatorio,
lava con luz el universo,
se acuesta a morir cada día
bajo las sábanas oscuras
de la noche germinadora
y para nacer otra vez
deja su huevo en el rocío.
Pido que mi resurrección
también sea reproductiva,
sea solar y delicada,
pero necesito dormir
en las sábanas de la luna
procreando modestamente
mis propias substancias terrestres.

Quiero extenderme en el vacío
desinteresado del viento
y propagarme sin descanso
en los cuarenta continentes,
nacer en formas anteriores,
ser camello, ser codorniz,
ser campanario en movimiento,
hoja del agua, gota de árbol,
araña, ballena del cielo
o novelista tempestuoso.

Ya sé que mi inmovilidad
es la garantía invisible
de todo el establecimiento:
si cambiamos de zoología
no nos admiten en el cielo.

ALWAYS BEING BORN

The sun grows from a seed
to its exigent splendor,
washes the world with its light,
lies down to die every day
under dark sheets
in the seminal night,
leaving its egg in the dew
to be born again in the morning.
I ask for the same resurrection,
solar, fastidious,
germinal after my fashion:
I would sleep
in the moon's linens,
a modest begetter, wed
to my own terrestrial substances.

I should like to enlarge on that vacancy
neutral as wind
beget myself over and over
in all forty continents;
be born in primordial guises
as camel or quail,
be a bell-tower in motion,
a leaf on the water, a waterdrop in a tree,
a spider, a whale in the sky,
a tempestuous novelist.

My immobility only
invests the old fixities
with invisible guarantees;
changing our zoology,
we forfeit our place in that heaven.

Pablo Neruda / 53

Por eso sentado en mi piedra
veo girar sobre mis sueños
los helicópteros que vuelven
de sus estrellas diminutas
y no necesito contarlos,
siempre hay algunos en exceso,
sobre todo en la primavera.

Y si me voy por los caminos
recurro al aroma olvidado
de una rosa deshabitada,
de una fragancia que perdí
como se extravía la sombra:
me quedé sin aquel amor
desnudo en medio de la calle.

Seated here on my rock, I see
helicopters, flying
diminutive stars,
whirl over my sleep.
No need to count—
there are always too many,
especially in Spring.

And if I take to the road,
the same forgotten aroma
of uninhabited roses comes back,
some fragrance I lost
as some lose their shadow:
and deprived of its love, I stand
stock-still, stark naked, in the middle of the street.

AYER

Todos los poetas excelsos
se reían de mi escritura
a causa de la puntuación,
mientras yo me golpeaba el pecho
confesando puntos y comas,
exclamaciones y dos puntos,
es decir, incestos y crímenes
que sepultaban mis palabras
en una Edad Media especial
de catedrales provincianas.

Todos los que nerudearon
comenzaron a vallejarse
y antes del gallo que cantó
se fueron con Perse y con Eliot
y murieron en su piscina.

Mientras tanto yo me enredaba
con mi calendario ancestral
más anticuado cada día
sin descubrir sino una flor
descubierta por todo el mundo,
sin inventar sino una estrella
seguramente ya apagada,
mientras yo embebido en su brillo,
borracho de sombra y de fósforo,
seguía el cielo estupefacto.

La próxima vez que regrese
con mi caballo por el tiempo
voy a disponerme a cazar
debidamente agazapado

YESTERDAY

All really superior poets
laugh at my penmanship—
because of the punctuation—
while I keep thumping my breast
confessing my commas and periods,
colons, exclamation points:
all the incestuous and criminal
acts that have buried my words
in a Dark Ages special to me
like provincial cathedrals.

Those who were lately *nerudarized*
are beginning to *vallejolate:*
before the cock crowed up the dawn
they settled for Eliot and Perse
and drowned in their fishpond.

Nevertheless, I go on spinning
my own ancestral time-table,
chintzier with each passing day,
without discovering so much as a flower
not already discovered by others
or inventing a single
fixed star not already extinct;
tipsy with all that incandescence,
smashed on the shadow and phosphor of things,
I keep searching a stupefied sky.

Next time I come back
into time, astride my habitual nag,
I'll give all my attention to stalking
anything that moves—in the sky, on the ground,

todo lo que corra o que vuele:
a inspeccionarlo previamente
si está inventado o no inventado,
descubierto o no descubierto:
no se escapará de mi red
ningún planeta venidero.

with the regulation hunterly crouch:
that way, ahead of the game, I can check
on what is or isn't invented already,
discovered, or still undiscovered:
nothing—not a planet unborn
in the gases—will slip past the knots of my net.

DIABLITOS

He visto cómo preparaba
su condición el oportuno,
su coartada el arribista,
sus redes la rica barata,
sus inclusiones el poeta.
Yo jugué con el papel limpio
frente a la luz todos los días.

Yo soy obrero pescador
de versos vivos y mojados
que siguen saltando en mis venas.
Nunca supe hacer otra cosa
ni supe urdir los menesteres
del intrínseco jactancioso
o del perverso intrigador,
y no es propaganda del bien
lo que estoy diciendo en mi canto:
sino que no lo supe hacer,
y le pido excusas a todos:
déjenme solo con el mar:
yo nací para pocos peces.

LITTLE DEVILS

I've seen them: the fixers
setting up their advantages,
the arriviste's alibis,
rich cheapskates spreading their nets,
poets drawing their boundaries;
but I've played with clean paper
in the open light of the day.

I'm a journeyman fisherman
of living wet verses
that break through the veins;
it's all I was good for.
I never contrived opportunities
out of mere vainglory
or a schemer's perversity;
whatever I say in my songs
is more than benign propaganda.
True, I did it all clumsily
and for that I beg pardon:
now leave me alone with my ocean:
I was born for a handful of fishes.

MORIR

Cómo apartarse de uno mismo
(sin desconocerse tampoco):
abrir los cajones vacíos,
depositar el movimiento,
el aire libre, el viento verde,
y no dejar a los demás
sino una elección en la sombra,
una mirada en ascensor
o algún retrato de ojos muertos?

De alguna manera oficial
hay que establecer una ausencia
sin que haya nada establecido,
para que la curiosidad
sienta una ráfaga en la cara
cuando destapen la oratoria
y hallen debajo de los pies
la llamarada del ausente.

DYING

How to remove oneself from oneself
(without unknowing oneself totally):
open the empty receptacles,
consign our mobility there,
the free air, the green wind,
and not leave for the rest
only an option of shadows,
a chance glance in an elevator,
a picture gone dead in the eyes?

Some protocol must be found
for establishing absence
with nothing really established
—some allowance for the curious among
us who feel the great gust in their faces
when the oratorical sound is uncovered,
and find, just under their boot-soles,
the absent one blazing back at them.

CAYENDO

Yo te llamo, rosa de leche,
duplicada paloma de agua,
ven desde aquella primavera
a resucitar en las sábanas,
a encender detrás del invierno
el sol erótico del día.

Hoy en mi propia circunstancia
soy un desnudo peregrino
viajando a la iglesia del mar:
crucé las piedras saladas,
seguí el discurso de los ríos
y me senté junto a la hoguera
sin saber que era mi destino.

Sobreviviente de la sal,
de las piedras y de las llamas,
sigo cruzando las regiones
sosteniéndome en mis dolores,
enamorado de mi sombra.
Por eso no por mucho andar
llego a alejarme de mí mismo.

Es este día mentiroso
de falsa luz encapotada,
lo que me puso macilento:
me caigo en *el tiempo del pozo*
y después de nadar debajo
de la inexacta primavera
salgo a la luz en cualquier parte
con el mismo sombrero gris
tocando la misma guitarra.

FALLING

Milk-rose, duplicate
dove of the water, I summon you:
come out of that Spring,
give new life to our linens,
fire the sun's rutting day
on the other side of our winter.

I speak for myself: today
I'm a nude pilgrim
on his way to the church of the sea:
I've crossed the salt stones,
followed the discourse of rivers,
sat close to the fire
without guessing my destiny.

Having survived all that brine,
the bonfires, the boulders,
I kept crossing the zones
with only my grief to sustain me,
in love with my shadow.
For all my meandering, in this sign
alone I've come to outdistance myself.

This whole lying day
furtive and false in its light,
I am drained of my strength:
I fall through *the time of the well*
paddling alone in the depths
of a Spring's inexactitude
till a part of me breaks toward the light,
wearing my same old gray hat,
with a thumb on the self-same guitar.

Pablo Neruda / 65

MAREJADA EN 1968. OCÉANO PACÍFICO

La marejada se llevó
todos los cercos de la orilla:
tal vez era el sueño del mar,
la dinamita del abismo:
la verdad es que no hay palabras
tan duras como el oleaje,
ni hay tantos dientes en el mundo
como en la cólera marina.

Cuando se enrolla la diadema
del mar y arrecian sus escudos
y las torres se levantaron,
cuando galopa con los pies
de mil millones de caballos
y la cabeza enfurecida
pega en la piedra del relámpago,
dice el pescador pequeñito
golpeándose el pecho mojado
para morir sin agonía.

Crispado mar, tortuga amarga,
panoplia del asesinato,
diapasón de la guerra a muerte,
piano de dientes carniceros,
hoy derribaste mis defensas
con un pétalo de tu furia
y como un ave crepitante
cantabas en los arrecifes.

Aquí está el mar, dicen los ojos,
pero hay que esperar una vida
para vivirlo hasta la muerte

HIGH SURF: THE PACIFIC (1968)

The surf carries away
the whole hoop of the beach:
a probable dream of the sea,
dynamite working the depths:
truth has no word
like the flint of these breakers,
and the teeth of the world
cannot equal its watery rage.

The sea that uncovers
its diadems and tempers its shields
lifts up towers,
gallops hard on the hooves
of millions of horses:
the head of a madman
strikes fire from the flint,
says the tiniest fisherman,
beating the wet of his breast
to lighten his death agony.

Convulsions, the tortoise's bitterness,
a murderer's panoply,
diapasons, wars to the death,
a piano of slaughterer's teeth—
you have swept my defenses away
with one petal of fury;
a hoarse cackle of sea-birds
sings on the reefs.

Here is the sea, say my eyes;
but my whole life was a vigil
to follow its power to the end

y te premia una tempestad
con cuatro gotas de granito.

En la Punta del Trueño anduve
recogiendo sal en el rostro
y del océano, en la boca
el corazón huracanado:
lo vi estallar hasta el cenit,
morder el cielo y escupirlo.

En cada ráfaga llevaba
el armamento de una guerra,
todas las lágrimas del mundo
y un tren repleto de leones,
pero no era bastante aún
y derribaba lo que hacía
despeñando sobre la piedra
una lluvia de estatuas frías.

Oh, firmamento del revés,
oh estrellas hirvientes del agua,
oh marejada del rencor,
dije, mirando la hermosura
de todo el mar desordenado
en una batalla campal
contra mi patria sacudida
por un temblor inexorable
y los designios de la espuma.

for a hurricane's recompense—
four drops of granite.

In Punte del Trueño I walked
facing the ocean, soaked
in its salt, a typhoon
alive in my mouth, like a heart:
I saw the zenith explode,
bite and spit out the sky with its teeth.

Each gust mounted
a warrior's armory,
a train of caged lions
and the tears of the world,
but nothing stood firm:
the breakers undid what they did,
smashing their way through the shoals
in a frieze of cold statues.

O upsidedown firmament
with stars boiling out of the water,
surf massing the weight of its angers,
I said, watching that loveliness:
the sea's total disorder
is another part of the field, the battle
goes on, and my shifting paternity
bends to the shock of what cannot be changed,
and the emblems that order the spray.

SEX

Se abrió tal vez el gineceo
en el año de nuestros años
y el sexo saltó las ventanas,
los ministerios y las puertas,
y vimos asomar los senos
en la celeste timidez
de las tarjetas postales
hasta que sobre el escenario
se deshojaron las mujeres
y una ola inmensa de desnudos
sobrepasó las catedrales.

Luego el comercio estableció
con libros, pantallas, revistas,
el imperio inmenso del culo
hasta inundar las poblaciones
con esperma industrializada.
Era difícil escapar
hacia el amor o tus trabajos,
te perseguían los ladridos
del sexo desencadenado
depositado en almacenes,
chorreando gotas mensajeras,
alcanzándote en los anuncios,
siguiéndote en la carretera
o regando hasta las aldeas
con su acueducto genital.

La literatura cruzó
este siglo de falo en falo
haciendo graciosas piruetas
o cayéndose de agonía

SEX

The harems have opened
in this year of our Lord
and Sex has jumped out of the windows,
the executive suites and the doors—
we've seen its breasts, bared
in celestial timidity
like the writing on post cards,
and women keep shedding
like petals in a lighted proscenium.
A great wave of nudes has rolled up
and crashed over the cathedrals.

The hustlers have come
with their books and their screens and revues—
a great Empire of Assholes
drowning the cities
with commercialized sperm.
It's hard to escape
to one's work or one's loves:
the wolf-whistle of promiscuous
sex, stored up in warehouses
or spurting its drops on the media,
hornily nips at our heels,
overtaking the newspaper ads,
tailing one on the freeways
or soaking the least of the villages
with its genital aqueduct.

Literature has crossed
into the century, phallus by phallus, with arabesque
turns on the point of its toes,
demeaning our anguish

y los libros que se ensuciaron
no cayeron en otra charca
que la del alma malherida.

Sépase que sin jardinero
fue más bello el jardin hirsuto,
pero una negra enredadera
enrolló su pelo de espanto
en los libros de la desdicha.

Y asi fue la página blanca,
que se parecía a la luna,
transformándose en patrimonio
de una tristísima impudicia.
Hasta que no tuvimos libros
para leer sino la luz
y cinco sílabas de sol
son una palabra desnuda
y la razón de la pureza.

with books—a backwash of filth, all
flooding one way to the sewers
of susceptible spirits.

The garden was good once
in its hairiness, without any gardeners;
but a black tangle of creepers
has unfolded the bush of its fear
in the books of the destitute.

The page that was white
and seemed blank as the moon
has changed its inheritance
for a grimace of dreary immodesty.
There are no longer books, only
lights to be read—
five syllables of sun,
one naked word
in the rational sign of our purity.

EL ENEMIGO

Hoy vino a verme un enemigo.
Se trata de un hombre encerrado
en su verdad, en su castillo,
como en una caja de hierro,
con su propia respiración
y las espadas singulares
que amamantó para el castigo.

Miré los años en su rostro,
en sus ojos de agua cansada,
en las líneas de soledad
que le subieron a las sienes
lentamente, desde el orgullo.

Hablamos en la claridad
de un medio día pululante,
con viento que esparcía sol
y sol combatiendo en el cielo.
Pero el hombre sólo mostró
las nuevas llaves, el camino
de todas las puertas. Yo creo
que adentro de él iba el silencio
que no podía compartirse.
Tenía una piedra en el alma:
él preservaba la dureza.

Pensé en su mezquina verdad
enterrada sin esperanza
de herir a nadie sino a él
y miré mi pobre verdad
maltratada adentro de mí.

THE ENEMY

My old enemy came to visit
today: a man hermetically sealed
in his truth, like a castle
or strong-box,
with his own style of breathing
and a singular sword-play
sedulously stropped to draw blood.

I saw the years in his face:
the eyes of tired water,
the lines of his loneliness
that had lifted his temples
little by little to consummate self-love.

We chatted a while in
broad mid-day, in windy
explosions that scattered
the sun on all sides and struck at the sky.
But the man showed me only
his new set of keys, his one
way to all doors. Inside him,
I think he was silent,
indivisibly silent:
the flint of his soul
stayed impenetrable.

I thought of that stingy integrity
hopelessly buried, with power
to harm only himself;
and within me I knew
my own crude truths shamed.

Pablo Neruda / 75

Allí estábamos cada uno
con su certidumbre afilada
y endurecida por el tiempo
comos dos ciegos que defienden
cada uno su oscuridad.

So we talked—each of us
honing his steely convictions,
each tempered by time:
two blind men defending
their individual darknesses.

CAMINANDO CAMINOS

De noche, por las carreteras
de la sequía, piedra y polvo,
tartamudea el carromato.

No pasa nadie por aquí.

El suelo no tiene habitantes
sino la aspereza encendida
por los faros vertiginosos:
es la noche de las espinas,
de los vegetales armados
como caimanes, con cuchillos:
se ven los dientes del alambre
alrededor de los potreros,
los cactus de hostil estatura
como obeliscos espinosos,
la noche seca, y en la sombra
llena de estrellas polvorientas
el nido negro de la aurora
que prepara sin descansar
los horizontes amarillos.

ON THE ROAD

At night, in the drought
of the highway, powder and pebble,
a cart stutters by.

No one passes this way.

The soil has no living inhabitant:
only a gritty asperity touched
into fire by vertiginous beacons:
this is the night of the nettles,
of vegetables armored
like alligators, with drawn daggers:
one sees only fanged wire ringing
the pasturage,
cactus, hostilely huge
and spiny as obelisks,
the parched night, and there in the dark
full of powdery stars,
the black nest of sunrise
readying again, without rest,
its yellow horizons.

CANCIÓN CON PAISAJE Y RÍO

De Villarrica los collados,
los rectángulos amarillos,
la fiesta verde horizontal,
las fucsias de boca violeta,
además del último orgullo
de los robles sobrevivientes
voy entrando en mi propia edad:
en las aguas que me nacieron.

A mí me dio a luz el golpe
de la lluvia entre los terrones
y nunca pude abrir los ojos
de par en par, como es debido:

yo me quedé semienterrado
como la simiente olvidada
y jugué con la oscuridad
sin olvidar los buenos días.

Ahora que se reintegran
a estas soledades mis huesos
varias veces vuelvo a nacer
por arte del sol tempestuoso
hundo en el pasto la cabeza,
tocan el cielo mis raíces.

A Villarrica por el río
Toltén Toltén Toltén Toltén.

SONG WITH LANDSCAPE AND A RIVER

The plateaus of Villarrica,
the rectangular yellows
and horizontal green banquets,
the fuchsias with violet mouths,
to the ultimate pride
of unkillable oak:
I enter my heritage,
the waters that gave me my life.

I was slapped into life
by the blow of the rain on a clod
and could never quite open
my eyes in the usual way.

I was always half-buried
like a seed left forgotten:
I played with the dark
without forgetting the good days.

My bones knit themselves
back in this solitude:
I'm born many times over
in the sun's cunning rage.
I bury my head in the meadow
and my roots touch the sky.

At Villarrica, there by the river
called Toltén, Toltén, Toltén, Toltén.

PAISAJE

Anduve diciéndole adiós
a muchos distantes, y ahora
me gustaría recoger
el hilo de aquellos adioses,
volver a ver ojos perdidos.

No sé si a todas les conviene
mi melancolía de hoy:
estoy dispuesto a repartirla
en pequeños granos redondos
alrededor del campamento,
en las rodillas del camino.
Quiero ver si crece la pena,
las flores de la incertidumbre,
la indecisión apesarada:
quiero saber de qué color
son las hojas del abandono.

Cuando un día te mira el sol
como un tigre desde su trono
y quiere obligarte a vivir
su condición voluntariosa,
recibo una racha lunática,
me desespero de sombrío,
y cuando menos lo esperaba
me pongo a repartir tristeza.

LANDSCAPE

I've kept waving goodbye
to the things that were moving away: now
I'd like to recover
the thread of those old valedictions
and look straight into the eye of my losses.

I can't say that my new melancholia
will be pleasing to many:
I'd rather divide what's mine
into little round pellets,
dropping crumbs in the lap of my path
as I tour the encampment:
I'd like to see if suffering
grows flowers of uncertainty
and corroding bewilderment:
I'd like to know for myself
what color the leaves of abandonment turn.

With the sun looking at us
one way like a tiger enthroned,
demanding a princely
volition to live from the human condition,
I get the craziest hunch of good things to come
and despair of my taciturn habits:
but now as expectancy lessens
I take sadness and share it with all.

ARTES POÉTICAS (I)

Como poeta carpintero
busco primero la madera
áspera o lisa, predispuesta:
con las manos toco el olor,
huelo el color, paso los dedos
por la integridad olorosa,
por el silencio del sistema,
hasta que me duermo o transmigro
o me desnudo y me sumerjo
en la salud de la madera:
en sus circunvalaciones.

Lo segundo que hago es cortar
con sierra de chisporroteo
la tabla recién elegida:
de la tabla salen los versos
como astillas emancipadas,
fragantes, fuertes y distantes
para que ahora mi poema
tenga piso, casco, carena,
se levante junto al camino,
sea habitado por el mar.

Como poeta panadero
preparo el fuego, la harina,
la levadura, el corazón,
y me complico hasta los codos
amasando la luz del horno,
el agua verde del idioma,
para que el pan que me sucede
se venda en la panadería.

Yo soy y no sé si lo sepan
tal vez herrero por destino

ARS POETICA (I)

As carpenter-poet, first
I fit the wood to my need—
on the knotty or satiny side:
then I savor the smell with my hands,
smell the colors, take the fragrant
entirety, the whole system
of silence, into my fingertips
and slip off to sleep, or transmigrate,
or strip to the skin and submerge
in woody well-being:
the wood's circumlocutions.

Then I cut into the board
of my choice
with the sputtering points of my saw:
from the plank come my verses,
like chips freed from the block,
sweet-smelling, swarthy, remote,
while the poem lays down its deck
and its hull, calculates list,
lifts up its bulk by the road
and the ocean inhabits it.

As baker: I prepare
what is needed—fire, flour,
leaven, the heart of the baker—
and wade in, to my elbows,
kneading the glow of the oven
into watery green language,
so the bread on the paddle
brings buyer to baker.

Or blacksmith, perhaps—
an affinity not granted by many:

o por lo menos propicié
para todos y para mí
metalúrgica poesía.

En tal abierto patrocinio
no tuve adhesiones ardientes:
fui ferretero solitario.

Rebuscando herraduras rotas
me trasladé con mis escombros
a otra región sin habitantes,
esclarecida por el viento.
Allí encontré nuevos metales
que fui convirtiendo en palabras.

Comprendo que mis experiencias
de metafísico manual
no sirvan a la poesía,
pero yo me dejé las uñas
arremetiendo a mis trabajos
y ésas son las pobres recetas
que aprendí con mis propias manos:
si se prueba que son inútiles
para ejercer la poesía
estoy de inmediato de acuerdo:
me sonrío para el futuro
y me retiro de antemano.

the least I require
of myself and my verse
is a metallurgical medium.

In this free confraternity
I've no burning allegiances.
I was always a lone iron-monger.

Keeping close watch on my broken
machinery, I move off with my junkpile
to some other uninhabited region
glossed by the wind.
There I dig for new metals
and turn what I am into words.

Granted: one poet's experience
with manual metaphysics
doesn't make a poetics;
but I've pared my nails to the quick
to temper my craft
and these shabby prescriptions
I learned for myself, at first hand:
if you find them uncouth
for a poet's vocation,
I agree—no apologies needed!
I smile toward the future
and am gone before you can give me your reasons.

SILENCIO

Yo que crecí dentro de un árbol
tendría mucho que decir,
pero aprendí tanto silencio
que tengo mucho que callar
y eso se conoce creciendo
sin otro goce que crecer,
sin más pasión que la substancia,
sin más acción que la inocencia,
y por dentro el tiempo dorado
hasta que la altura lo llama
para convertirlo en naranja.

SILENCE

Though I grew up in a tree
and should have something to say on the matter,
I have learned such great silence
that my deepest wish now is to be still.
I know this by growing
in the sheer joy of growing,
the passion that inheres in all substance,
the action that lives in its innocence.
Time goes golden inside
and waits till height calls to it there
and all is turned into an orange.

UNIDAD

Esta hoja son todas las hojas,
esta flor son todos los pétalos
y una mentira la abundancia.
Porque todo fruto es el mismo,
los árboles son uno solo
y es una sola flor la tierra.

UNITY

All leaves are this leaf,
all petals, this flower
in a lie of abundance.
All fruit is the same,
the trees are only one tree
and one flower sustains all the earth.

CAE LA FLOR

Los siete pétalos del mar
se juntan en esta corola
con la diadema del amor:
Sucedió todo en el vaivén
de una rosa que cayó al agua
cuando el río llegaba al mar.
Así un borbotón escarlata
saltó del día enamorado
a los mil labios de la ola
y una rosa se deslizó
hacia el sol y sobre la sal.

A FALLING FLOWER

The sea's seven petals
join in a single corolla
and are love's diadem:
All comes to pass in the valve
of a rose that fell to the water
when the river came down to the sea.
One scarlet bubble
leapt from the loves of the day
toward a thousand lips in the wave,
and a rose glided
sunward on salt.

AGUA

La desventaja del rocío
cuando su luz se multiplica
es que a la flor le nacen ojos
y estos ojos miran el mundo.

Ya dejaron de ser rocío.

Son las circunstancias del día:
reflexiones de la corola:
eternidad del agua eterna.

WATER

The dew's disadvantage
in a multiple light
is that eyes are born in the flower
and the eyes look out at the world:

they are dewdrops no longer.

They are day's circumstances:
the corolla's reflections:
water's eternity, eternally there.

RAZÓN

La oblonga razón de la rama
parece inmóvil pero escucha
cómo suena la luz del cielo
en la cítara de sus hojas
y si te inclinas a saber
cómo sube el agua a la flor
oirás la luna cantar
en la noche de las raíces.

REASON

The oblong reason of the bough
seems unmoved to us; yet it hears
light's sound in the sky
in a zither of leaves;
and if you lean closer to learn
how water climbs in the flower
you'll hear the moon sing
in the night of the roots.

ÁRBOL

Anoche al apagar la luz
se me durmieron las raíces
y se me quedaron los ojos
enredados entre las hojas
hasta que, tarde, con la sombra
se me cayó una rama al sueño
y por el tronco me subió
la fría noche de cristal
como una iguana transparente.

Entonces me quedé dormido.

Cerré los ojos y las hojas.

TREE

When I switched off the lights last night
all my roots went to sleep
while my eyes remained
caught in the leafage:
later, with dark flooding in,
a branch fell over my dream:
the cold night rose
from the trunk, crystal-clear,
a transparent iguana.

I slept soundly then.

I closed my eyes and my leaves.

ANIMAL

Aquel certero escarabajo
voló con élitros abiertos
hasta la cereza infrarroja.

La devoró sin comprender
la química del poderío
y luego volvió a los follajes
convertido en un incendiario.

Su corazón derivó
como un cometa saturado
por la radiación deliciosa
y se fue ardiendo en la substancia
de tan quemantes electrones:

al disolverse alcanzó a ser
un síntoma del arco-iris.

ANIMAL

That sharpshooting beetle
flew with wide-open wing-cases
toward the infra-red cherry.

He devoured it, unaware
of the chemistry of power
and came back to the foliage,
a consummate incendiary.

His heart made its descent
like a comet soaked
in the rich radiation
and he went away scorched with the stuff
of those blazing electrons:

and dissolving, accomplished
a symptom of rainbows.

ABEJAS (I)

Qué voy a hacerle, yo nací
cuando habían muerto los dioses
y mi insufrible juventud
siguió buscando entre las grietas:
ése fue mi oficio y por eso
me sentí tan abandonado.

Una abeja más una abeja
no suman dos abejas claras
no dos abejas oscuras:
suman un sistema de sol,
una habitación de topacio,
una caricia peligrosa.

La primera inquietud del ámbar
son dos abejas amarillas
y atado a las mismas abejas
trabaja el sol de cada día:
me da rabia enseñarles tanto
de mis ridículos secretos.

Me van a seguir preguntando
mis relaciones con los gatos,
cómo descubrí el arco iris,
por qué se vistieron de erizos
las beneméritas castañas,
y sobre todo que les diga
lo que piensan de mí los sapos,
los animales escondidos
bajo la fragancia del bosque
o en las pústulas del cemento.

BEES: I

What could I do? I was born
when the gods had all died,
and my incorrigible childhood
was spent looking between all the crevices:
that was my function: that's
why I'm left out of it now.

One bee plus one bee
does not make two light bees
or two dark bees:
they make up a cycle of sun,
a mansion of topaz,
a hazardous touching of hands.

The initial disturbance in amber
requires two yellow bees:
around them the quotidian sun
toils in its orbit:
I'm wild to explain
my ridiculous secrets.

But they keep after me
with their questions: what are my relations
with cats, how I discovered the rainbow,
why the worth of the chestnut
is contained in its burr;
they want, of all things, to know
the bullfrog's opinions: what do
animals under their burrows
in the fragrance of forests or
in pustules of asphalt, make of my life?

Pablo Neruda / 103

Es la verdad que entre los sabios
he sido el único ignorante
y entre los que menos sabían
yo siempre supe un poco menos
y fue tan poco mi saber
que aprendí la sabiduría.

The truth of it is: of all
extant sages, I alone remained ignorant,
and among those who have learned less and less
I was always a jot less in the know—
till my learning has come to so little
I know how to be wise, in the end.

ABEJAS (II)

Hay un cementerio de abejas
allá en mi tierra, en Patagonia,
y vuelven con su miel a cuestas
a morir de tanta dulzura.

Es una región tempestuosa
curvada como una ballesta
con un permanente arco iris
como una cola de faisán:
rugen los saltos de los ríos,
salta la espuma como liebre,
restalla el viento y se dilata
por la soledad circundante:
es un círculo la pradera
con la boca llena de nieve
y la barriga colorada.

Allí llegan una por una,
un millón junto a otro millón,
a morir todas las abejas
hasta que la tierra se llena
de grandes montes amarillos.

No puedo olvidar su fragancia.

BEES: II

There's a graveyard of bees
back in my country, in Patagonia:
bees with bowed back of honey
come to die in the sweetness.

A storm-battered place:
curved like a crossbow
with a permanent rainbow
like the light in a pheasant's tail:
waterfalls roar in the rivers,
foam leaps like a hare,
wind crackles and widens its passage
in the encompassing solitude:
the whole meadow circles
with its mouth full of snow
and the pink mound of its belly.

The bees come to die there, first
one after one, then
millions on millions,
till the whole earth is piled
with their great yellow mountains.

I shall never forget their aroma.

PERRO

Los perros desinteresados
por los caminos, sin regreso,
por el polvo errante, a la luz
de la intemperie indiferente.

Oh Dios de los perros perdidos,
pequeño dios de patas tristes,
acércate a nuestro hemisferio
de largas colas humilladas,
de ojos hambrientos que persiguen
a la luna color de hueso!

Oh Dios descuidado, yo soy
poeta de las carreteras
y vago en vano sin hallar
un idioma de perrería
que los acompañe cantando
por la lluvia o la polvareda.

DOG

The dogs, indifferent to roads
leading one way only
through haphazard dust to the light
of a lackluster weather:

Oh, God of lost dogs,
little god of the woebegone paws,
come close to our hemisphere
of long, humbled tails
and famishing eyes that point
to a bone-colored moon!

O negligent God, I'm
a poet of highways and byways and sorts
floundering vainly to find
a language of dogdom
that stays with all dogs to the end
and bays in the dust-cloud and storm.

OTRO PERRO

Perseguí por aquellas calles
a un perro errante, innecesario,
para saber adónde van
de noche trotando los perros.

Sólo mil veces se detuvo
a orinar en sitios remotos
y siguió como si tuviera
que recibir un telegrama.

Pasó casas y cruzó esquinas,
parques, aldeas y países,
y yo detrás del caminante
para saber adónde iba.

Siguió sin fin sobrepasando
los barrios llenos de basura,
los puentes desiertos e inútiles
cuando dormían los carruajes.

Los regimientos, las escuelas,
las estatuas de bronce muerto,
la tristeza de los prostíbulos
y los cabarets fatigados,
cruzamos, el perro adelante
y yo, cansado como un perro.

ANOTHER DOG

Street after street, I kept trailing
the old dog's meanders, for no better reason
than to know where dogs go
in their tour of the night.

A thousand times, by my count, he stopped
to pee in odd places,
then went on with the air of
someone expecting a telegram.

He passed houses, crossed corners,
parks, villages, countries,
while I followed behind him to know
where dogs needed to go.

He endlessly pottered along,
putting barrios of garbage behind him,
empty bridges, of no use
while the carriages slept.

Whole regiments, schools,
the statues' dead bronzes,
a pathos of brothels,
and tired cabarets: we crossed
them all off, the dog leading the way,
and I at his heels, dog-tired.

PEZ

Aquel pez negro de Acapulco
me miró con ojos redondos
y regresó a la transparencia
de su océano de anilina:
vi sus bigotes despedir
unas cuantas gotas de mar
que resplandecieron, celestes.

Y cuando cayó de mi anzuelo
volviendo al susurro entreabierto
de la piedra y del agua azul
no había en sus ojos estáticos
reconocimiento ninguno
hacia la tierra, ni hacia el hombre.

Yo me sacudí de reír
por mi fracaso y por su cara
y él se deslizó a revivir
sin emociones, en el agua.

FISH

The black Acapulcan fish
that stared me down with round eyes
and sank back into ocean's
indigo dyes of transparency:
I saw how his mustache struck off
a few drops of the sea
and flashed a divine coruscation.

He fell from my tackle,
restored to the half-open yawn
of the stones and blue sea-water;
his fanatical eyes
gave no sign of acknowledgment
to earth or to man.

I fought back an impulse to laugh
at his face and my failure,
and he slipped back to life
in the water, unmoved to the last.

BESTIARIO (I)

El antílope clandestino
se desarrolla en la fogata:
Su hocico se nutre de fuego
y su cola parece de humo.

Van y vienen las llamaradas
por la corona cornamenta
y el animal, fiel a su signo,
resuelve el extraño sistema
de los ardientes alimentos
dejando como puntuaciones
detrás de su cola quemada
un collar tácito de ámbar.

BESTIARY: I

The clandestine antelope
discloses himself in a holocaust:
His muzzle feeds on the fire
and his tail evanesces like smoke.

Flares come and go
in the horn of that crown,
while the animal, true to his kind,
resolves the strange pattern
of his food's calefaction,
leaving behind him, like punctuation,
under the blazon of tail,
his tacit necklace of amber.

OTOÑO

Para la patria del topacio
designé una espiga infinita
y le agregué la ramazón
de la estirpe más amarilla:

Son mis deberes en otoño.

AUTUMN

For that country of topaz
I invented an infinite kernel
of wheat and added a thicket
of yellowest heraldry:

These are my autumn's responsibilities.

FUNDACIONES

Llegué tan temprano a este mundo
que escogí un país inconcluso
donde aún no se conocían
los noruegos ni los tomates:
las calles estaban vacías
como si ya se hubieran ido
los que aún no habian llegado,
y aprendí a leer en los libros
que nadie había escrito aún:
no habían fundado la tierra
donde yo me puse a nacer.

Cuando mi padre hizo su casa
comprendí que no comprendía
y había construido un árbol:
era su idea del confort.

Primero viví en la raíz,
luego en el follaje aprendí
poco a poco a volar más alto
en busca de aves y manzanas.
No sé cómo no tengo jaula,
ni voy vestido de plumero
cuando pasé toda mi infancia
paseándome de rama en rama.

Luego fundamos la ciudad
con exceso de callejuelas,
pero sin ningún habitante:
invitábamos a los zorros,
a los caballos, a las flores,
a los recuerdos ancestrales.

FOUNDATIONS

Coming early into the world
I chose an ambiguous country
where no one had heard
of tomatoes or Norwegians:
the streets were deserted
as if those yet to arrive
had already moved off,
and I learned how to read
from books still to be written:
the country remained unconfirmed
when I arrived to be born.

When my father decided to build,
I see now, he misunderstood:
he built us a tree—
it was his idea of comfort.

First I kept to the roots,
then I learned from the foliage
how to fly higher, little by little,
looking for apples and birds.
To this day I should live in a cage
and dress up in feathers,
having spent all my childhood
strolling from one branch to the next.

Later we founded a city
with a crosspatch of lanes
but no single inhabitant:
we invited the wolves
and the horses, the flowers,
the ancestral remembrances.

Pablo Neruda / 119

En vano en vano todo aquello:

no encontramos a nadie nunca
con quien jugar en una esquina.

Así fue de feliz mi infancia
que no se arregla todavía.

Useless, all of it useless!

We found no one to play with,
no one at all on the street corners.

Such were my childhood's delights—
and nothing has tidied up since.

EL QUE BUSCÓ

Salí a encontrar lo que perdí
en las ciudades enemigas:
me cerraban calles y puertas,
me atacaban con fuego y agua,
me disparaban excrementos.
Yo sólo quería encontrar
juguetes rotos en los sueños,
un caballito de cristal
o mi reloj desenterrado.

Nadie quería comprender
mi melancólico destino,
mi desinterés absoluto.

En vano expliqué a las mujeres
que no quería robar nada,
ni asesinar a sus abuelas.
Daban gritos de miedo al ver
que yo salía de un armario
o entraba por la chimenea.

Sin embargo, por largos días
y noches de lluvia violeta
mantuve mis expediciones:
furtivamente atravesé
a través de techos y tejas
aquellas mansiones hostiles
y hasta debajo de la alfombra
luché y luché contra el olvido.

Nunca encontré lo que buscaba.

SOMEONE LOOKING FOR THINGS

I went out to find what I lost
in the enemy cities:
they closed off the thresholds and streets,
attacked me with water and fire
and volleys of turds.
My wants were all simple:
playthings broken in dreams,
a cut-crystal pony,
my watch dug up from its grave.

Nobody wanted to understand
my taciturn destiny
or my total indifference.

Look, ladies, I said,
I'm not here to rob you
or murder your grandmother.
But the sight of me coming
out of a clothes-closet or climbing down
chimneys was enough: they yelled bloody murder.

Still and all, I kept on
with my old expeditions,
day-long or in nights of violet rain.
I pushed furtively forward, broke
and entered the roof-tiles
of inimical mansions,
fought my way under the mattresses
to conquer oblivion.

I never found what I was looking for.

Pablo Neruda / 123

Nadie tenía mi caballo,
ni mis amores, ni la rosa
que perdí como tantos besos
en la cintura de mi amada.

Fui encarcelado y malherido,
incomprendido y lesionado
como un malhechor evidente
y ahora no busco mi sombra.
Soy tan serio como los otros,
pero me falta lo que amé:
el follaje de la dulzura
que se desprende hoja por hoja
hasta que te quedas inmóvil,
verdaderamente desnudo.

Nobody has lassoed my horse
or my loves or the roses
I lost, like so many kisses,
in the waist of my lover.

I was locked up and beat up,
scarred, and misunderstood
for the obvious delinquent I was.
I no longer go looking for shadows.
I'm as sober as the next fellow,
mind you; but I've missed out on something I loved:
the whole foliage intact in its sweetness,
the falling to pieces of the foliage, leaf after leaf,
till, stopped in your tracks, you're left
as you were, stripped to the skin, fundamental.

CONDICIONES

Con tantas tristes negativas
me despedí de los espejos
y abandoné mi profesión:
quise ser ciego en una esquina
y cantar para todo el mundo
sin ver a nadie porque todos
se me parecían un poco.

Pero buscaba mientras tanto
cómo mirarme hacia detrás,
hacia donde estaba sin ojos
y era oscura mi condición.
No saqué nada con cantar
como un ciego del populacho:
mientras más amarga la calle
me parecía yo más dulce.

Condenado a quererme tanto
me hice un hipócrita exterior
ocultando el amor profundo
que me causaban mis defectos.
Y así sigo siendo feliz
sin que jamás se entere nadie
de mi enfermedad insondable:
de lo que sufrí por amarme
sin ser, tal vez, correspondido.

CONDITIONS

With these moody negations
I said goodbye to the mirrors
and gave up my profession:
better a blind man in a corner
singing songs to the world
without setting eyes on a soul,
if part of me is so like the others!

Nevertheless I kept trying:
how to look back at oneself
to wherever it is one sat blinded
when one's total condition was dark?
There was nothing to show for my singing
in a blind rabble of singers:
but the harsher the street sounds became,
the sweeter I seemed to myself.

Condemned to self-love,
I lived the exterior life of a hypocrite
hiding the depths of the love
my defects had brought down on my head.
I keep on being happy,
disclosing to nobody
my ambiguous malady:
the grief I endure for self-love,
who was never so loved in return.

SIEMPRE YO

Yo que quería hablar del siglo
adentro de esta enredadera,
que es mi siempre libro naciente,
por todas partes me encontré
y se me escapaban los hechos.
Con buena fe que reconozco
abrí los cajones al viento,
los armarios, los cementerios,
los calendarios con sus meses
y por las grietas que se abrían
se me aparecía mi rostro.

Por más cansado que estuviera
de mi persona inaceptable
volvía a hablar de mi persona
y lo que me parece peor
es que me pintaba a mí mismo
pintando un acontecimiento.
Qué idiota soy dije mil veces
al practicar con maestría
las descripciones de mi mismo
como si no hubiera habido
nada mejor que mi cabeza,
nadie mejor que mis errores.

Quiero saber, hermanos míos,
dije en la Unión de pescadores,
si todos se aman como yo.
La verdad es —me contestaron—
que nosotros pescamos peces
y tú te pescas a ti mismo
y luego vuelves a pescarte
y a tirarte al mar otra vez.

ME AGAIN

I who wanted to talk
of a century inside the web
that is always my poem-in-progress,
have found only myself wherever I looked
and missed the real happening.
With wary good faith
I opened myself to the wind: the lockers,
clothes-closets, graveyards,
the calendar months of the year,
and in every opening crevice
my face looked back at me.

The more bored I became
with my unacceptable person,
the more I returned to the theme of my person;
worst of all,
I kept painting myself to myself
in the midst of a happening.
What an idiot (I said to myself
a thousand times over) to perfect all that craft
of description and describe only myself,
as though I had nothing to show but my head,
nothing better to tell than the mistakes of a lifetime.

Tell me, good brothers,
I said at the Fishermen's Union,
do you love yourselves as I do?
The plain truth of it is:
we fishermen stick to our fishing,
while you fish for yourself (said
the fishermen): you fish over and over again
for yourself, then throw yourself back in the sea.

Pablo Neruda / 129

EL SIGLO MUERE

Treinta y dos años entrarán
trayendo el siglo venidero,
treinta y dos trompetas heroicas,
treinta y dos fuegos derrotados,
y el mundo seguirá tosiendo
envuelto en su sueño y su crimen.

Tan pocas hojas que le faltan
al árbol de las amarguras
para los cien años de otoño
que destruyeron el follaje:
lo regaron con sangre blanca,
con sangre negra y amarilla,
y ahora quiere una medalla
en su pechera de sargento
el siglo que cumple cien años
de picotear ojos heridos
con sus herramientas de hierro
y sus garras condecoradas.

Me dice el cemento en la calle,
me canta el pájaro enramado,
me advierte la cárcel nombrando
los justos allí ajusticiados,
me lo declaran mis parientes,
mis intranquilos compañeros,
secretarios de la pobreza:
siguen podridos estos años
parados en medio del tiempo
como los huesos de una res
que devoran los roedores
y salen de la pestilencia
libros escritos por las moscas.

A CENTURY DYING

Thirty-two years to go
to the new century:
thirty-two heroical fanfares,
thirty-two fires to stamp out
while the world goes coughing up phlegm,
wrapped in its dreams and atrocities.

The tree of our bitterness
has come full leaf:
and the fall of our century
will carry the foliage away:
we watered the roots with our white blood
and yellow and black;
now our centennial epoch
after scarring our vision
with cast-iron hardware
and armorial claws
wants medals to pin
on its sergeant's insignia.

The cement in the street says it,
a bird whistles it out of the branches,
the jails with their rosters
of good men maligned
make it plain to me; my kin,
my irascible friends,
the stewards of poverty,
put it in so many words:
the epoch is rotting away,
stalled at time's center
like the bones of a cow
with its predators gnawing within,
while out of time's pestilence
comes a literature written by flies.

Pablo Neruda / 131

REGRESANDO

A diez días de viaje largo
y desprovisto de opiniones
vuelvo a mi ser, a ser yo mismo,
el societario solitario
que pide siempre la palabra
para retener el derecho
de quedarse luego callado.

Resulta que llego otra vez
al centro inmóvil de mi mismo
desde donde nunca salí
y como en un reloj dormido
veo la hora verdadera:
la que se detiene una vez
no para inducir a la muerte,
sino para abrirte la vida.

Sucede que me moví tanto
que mis huesos se despertaban
en pleno sueño, caminando
hacia arrabales que crucé,
mercados que me sostuvieron,
escuelas que me perseguían,
aviones bajo la tormenta,
plazas llenas de gente urgente
y sobre mi alma que sin duda
se puso a dormir su fatiga
mi cuerpo continuó los viajes
con la vibración trepidante
de un camión repleto de piedras
que machacaba mi esqueleto.

COMING BACK

Ten days on the road,
fresh out of opinions,
I'm back to myself, to being
myself—the gregarious loner
who occasionally asks for the floor
to guard his prerogative
of keeping his own counsel.

I'm back again
at the immovable center of myself
(which I never really abandoned)
like a watch gone to sleep,
to tell you the time of the day—
the day that is given us once
not to hatch our own deaths,
but to hold our lives open.

I've been rattled about from this place
to that so often, my bones seem awake
when I'm sodden with sleep: I keep walking
and crossing the barrios,
the replenishing markets,
schools that pursued me,
planes under the eye of the storm,
plazas of exigent people:
back and forth, on a soul that ought surely to
sleep off its exhaustion somewhere,
my body continues its journeys,
with the crunching vibration
of a truck hauling stones,
chewing away at my skeleton.

A ver, alma, resucitemos
el punto en que se saludaron
el horario y el minutero:
ésa es la rendija del tiempo
para salir de la desdicha
y penetrar en la frescura.

(Allí hay un estanque infinito
hecho con láminas iguales
de transcurso y de transparencia
y no necesito mover
los cinco dedos de una mano
para recoger mis dolores
o la naranja prometida.)

De tanto volver a ese punto
comprendí que no necesito
tantos caminos para andar,
ni tantas sílabas externas,
ni tanto hombres ni mujeres,
ni tantos ojos para ver.

Parece —yo no lo aseguro—
que basta con ese minuto
que se detiene y precipita
lo que llevabas inconcluso
y no importa tu perfección,
ni tu ansiedad diseminada
en polvorientos derroteros:
Basta con bajar a ver
el silencio que te esperaba
y sientes que van a llegarte
las tentaciones del otoño,
las invitaciones del mar.

Let's see, I say to my soul: let's
resuscitate things at the point where the hour
and the minute hands salute one another:
the point where time's armor cracks
open, bad luck trickles away,
and one touches the freshness of things.

(There, one comes on a bottomless well—
transparency flowing away
in a gloss of identical planes;
there, without moving
so much as a finger
I can salvage all sorrow
and recover the pledge of an orange.)

After so many returns to a point
I see: one can walk
well enough without so many highways,
so many exterior syllables,
so many men or so many women
or so many eyes to see out of.

It comes to this: a moment
suffices, perhaps, to hold back
or push forward all that
we carry around inconclusively—
never mind your perfection,
or your anxious comings and goings
in the dust of the highways and byways.
Come down the best way you can, look
into the silence that waits for you now,
and the fullness of time will be given:
the autumn's enticements
and the ocean that beckons you, there.

VOLVER VOLVIENDO

Sacude el camino cortando
heroicas flores amarillas
y sigue apartando los cerros
abriendo el cielo a borbotones:
voy hacia lejos otra vez,
a la humedad enmarañada
de las cumbres de Nahuelbuta
y en el titánico transcurso
crece en mi ropa la distancia
y me voy haciendo camino.

Atravesando cordilleras
sin saber como se afiló
mi frente longitudinal
y saqué los pies de la tierra
para que no fueran raíces,
sino festín del movimiento.

El día izquierdo olvidará
la rosa rápida y perdida
antes de ser inaugurada,
porque debo llegar temprano
a mis lejanas circunstancias,
a saber lo que deja el río
en la insistencia de la orilla
con tantas palabras de piedra
como los pelos de un caballo.

La carretera corre abajo
hacia tal vez, hacia Coyhaique,
donde el agua se desarrolla
como el violín en un lamento.

RETURNING AGAIN

The way lurches forward, cutting
yellow, heroical flowers,
then goes on dividing the peaks
and breaking the sky into intervals:
My way is a far one again
through a briny humidity
to the heights of Nahuelbuta:
distance feeds on my clothing
as I climb the titanic perspective
and put the road past me.

Upland, crossing the ranges,
my longitudinal forehead
turns razor-sharp—heaven knows how—
earth moves away from my feet,
no longer planted like roots,
but an orgy of motion.

Veering off to the left, day
will forget its failed, flying rose
lost before even begun:
all is set for my early arrival
at a faraway circumstance:
to know what the river rejects
at the beach's insistence,
with stone words
matted like horse-hair.

The road hurtles below
toward—it may be—toward Coyhaique:
the water unfolds
like a fiddle's lament;

Y tengo patria más allá
donde corre el avestruz verde
contra las ráfagas navales
y comienza el reino sin dioses
donde el hielo es la claridad.

beyond lies my country—a place
where green ostriches race
through squalls blowing up from the sea,
the godless domain that begins
where all ice is clarity.

III: *Las piedras del cielo* / Stones of the Sky
(1970)

DE ENDURECER LA TIERRA

De endurecer la tierra
se encargaron las piedras:
pronto
tuvieron alas:
las piedras
que volaron:
las que sobrevivieron
subieron
el relámpago,
dieron un grito en la noche,
un signo de agua,
una espada violeta,
un meteoro.

El cielo
suculento
no sólo tuvo nubes,
no sólo espacio con olor a oxígeno,
sino una piedra terrestre
aquí y allá, brillando,
convertida en paloma,
convertida en campana,
en magnitud, en viento
penetrante:
en fosfórica flecha, en sal del cielo.

TO HARDEN THE EARTH

To harden the earth
is a stone's occupation—
till stone became
winged
and flew.
Those that survived
climbed
the lightning,
cried out
in the dark:
a watery token,
the violet light on a blade,
a meteor.

Our succulent
sky
holds more than the clouds
and the void, with its odor of oxygen—
it holds a terrestrial stone,
it flashes out here and there
with its look of a dove
or a bell,
takes on magnitude,
the cutting edge of the wind:
an arrow in the phosphorus, a facet of salt on the sky.

SE CONCENTRA EL SILENCIO

Se concentra el silencio
en una piedra,
los círculos se cierran,
el mundo tembloroso,
guerras, pájaros, casas,
ciudades, trenes, bosques,
la ola que repite las preguntas del mar,
el sucesivo viaje de la aurora,
llega a la piedra, nuez del cielo,
testigo prodigioso.

La piedra polvorienta en un camino
conoce a Pedro y sus antecedentes,
conoce el agua desde que nació:
es la palabra muda de la tierra:
no dice nada porque es la heredera
del silencio anterior, del mar inmóvil,
de la tierra vacía.

Allí estaba la piedra antes del viento,
antes del hombre y antes de la aurora:
su primer movimiento
fue la primera música del río.

SILENCE PACKS ITSELF

Silence packs itself
into stone:
the great circles close
and a whole, tremulous world
with its wars, birds, houses,
trains, forests, cities,
the wave that repeats the enigmas of ocean,
the consecutive journey of dawn—
all come to stone, the nut of the firmament,
to offer their witnesses.

The stone in the dust of the road
knows the old generations of Pedro,
the water that broke at his birth,
the mute word of earth:
it inherits primordial silence,
the sea's immobility,
the void of creation, and has nothing to say.

Before man was, or dawn, before
wind was, stone was:
the first movement of stone
and the music of rivers
were one.

CUANDO SE TOCA EL TOPACIO

Cuando se toca el topacio
el topacio te toca:
despierta el fuego suave
como si el vino en la uva
despertara.
Aún antes de nacer, el vino claro
adentro de una piedra
busca circulación, pide palabras,
entrega su alimento misterioso,
comparte el beso de la piel humana:
el contacto sereno
de piedra y ser humano
encienden una rápida corola
que vuelve luego a ser lo que antes era:
carne y piedra: entidades enemigas.

TOUCHING THE TOPAZ

Touching topaz,
one is touched by the topaz:
a bland fire awakens
as grapes are awakened
by wine.
Before coming to be, the clear wine
works in the stone:
it seeks circulation, wants words,
bears a mystical nutriment.
It shares the human kiss of the skin;
the power of that meeting,
the stone and its human observer,
blazes out in a headlong corolla;
subsides, and reveals what it was:
flesh and stone in their solitudes: enemy entities.

EL CUADRADO AL CRISTAL
LLEGA CAYENDO

El cuadrado al cristal llega cayendo
desde su simetría:
aquel que abre las puertas de la tierra
halla en la oscuridad, claro y completo,
la luz de este sistema transparente.

El cubo de la sal, los triangulares
dedos del cuarzo: el agua lineal
de los diamantes: el laberinto
del azufre y su gótico esplendor:
adentro de la nuez de la amatista
la multiplicación de los rectángulos:
todo esto hallé debajo de la tierra:
geometría enterrada:
escuela de la sal: orden del fuego.

THE SQUARE IN THE CRYSTAL FALLS

The square in the crystal falls
back in its symmetry:
those who open the doors of the earth
will find in the darkness, intact and complete,
the light of that system's transparency.

The salt cube, the triangular
fingers of quartz: the diamond's
linear water: the maze
in the sapphire and its gothic magnificence:
the multiplication of rectangles
in the nut of the amethyst:
all wait for us under the ground:
a whole buried geometry:
the salt's school: the decorum of fire.

HAY QUE HABLAR CLARO
DE LAS PIEDRAS CLARAS

Hay que hablar claro de las piedras claras,
de las piedras oscuras,
de la roca ancestral, del rayo azul
que quedó prisionero en el zafiro,
del peñasco estatuario en su grandeza
irregular, del vuelo submarino,
de la esmeralda con su incendio verde.

Ahora bien, el guijarro
o la mercadería fulgurante,
el relámpago virgen del rubí
o la ola congelada de la costa
o el secreto azabache que escogió
el brillo negativo de la sombra,
pregunto yo, mortal, perecedero,
de qué madre llegaron, de qué esperma
volcánica, oceánica, fluvial,
de qué flora anterior, de cuál aroma,
interrumpido por la luz glacial?
Yo soy de aquellos hombres transitorios
que huyendo del amor en el amor
se quedaron quemados, repartidos
en carne y besos, en palabras negras
que se comió la sombra:
no soy capaz para tantos misterios:
abro los ojos y no veo nada:
toco la tierra y continúo el viaje
mientras fogata o flor, aroma o agua,
se transforman en razas de cristal,
se eternizan en obras de la luz.

SPEAK PLAINLY OF STONE

Speak plainly of stone—the bright
and the dark of it—
rock's ancestry, the blue spark
imprisoned in sapphire,
the monument in the crag with its ragged
pomposity, the submarine flight
of the emerald in incendiary green.

Consider: the cobblestone's
glowering merchandise,
the virginal flash of the ruby,
the coastline congealed in a wave,
or the jet that elected
the negative glosses of darkness in secret.
Perishing mortal, I ask:
what mother delivered them, what
seed, oceanic, volcanic, alluvial,
what anterior flower or aroma
preempted by glacial light?
I speak as a transitive man:
caught between loves I am scorched by
a love, divided
by kisses and flesh, by black words
devoured by a shadow.
Unsuited for mysteries,
I open my eyes and see nothing:
I touch earth and resume my meander
among bonfires, flowers, aromas, water
transformed into races of crystal
or eternized as offspring of light.

EL LIQUEN EN LA PIEDRA

El liquen en la piedra, enredadera
de goma verde, enreda
el más antiguo jeroglífico,
extiende la escritura
del océano
en la roca redonda.
La lee el sol, la muerden los moluscos,
y los peces resbalan
de piedra en piedra como escalofríos.
En el silencio sigue el alfabeto
completando los signos sumergidos
en la cadera clara de la costa.

El liquen tejedor con su madeja
va y viene sube y sube
alfombrando la gruta de aire y agua
para que nadie baile sino la ola
y no suceda nada sino el viento.

LICHEN ON STONE

Lichen on stone: the web
of green rubber
weaves an old hieroglyphic,
unfolding the script
of the sea
on the curve of a boulder.
The sun reads it. The mollusk devours it.
Fish slither
on stone, with a bristling of hackles.
An alphabet moves in the silence,
printing its drowned incunabula
on the naked flank of the beaches.

The lichens
climb higher, plaiting and braiding, piling
their nap in the caverns of ocean and air, coming
and going, until nothing may dance but the wave
and nothing persist but the wind.